The Bill Gates Story

Tom Christian

Level 5

IBC パブリッシング

はじめに

　ラダーシリーズは、「はしご（ladder）」を使って一歩一歩上を目指すように、学習者の実力に合わせ、無理なくステップアップできるよう開発された英文リーダーのシリーズです。
　リーディング力をつけるためには、繰り返したくさん読むこと、いわゆる「多読」がもっとも効果的な学習法であると言われています。多読では、「1. 速く　2. 訳さず英語のまま　3. なるべく辞書を使わず」に読むことが大切です。スピードを計るなど、速く読むよう心がけましょう（たとえば TOEIC® テストの音声スピードはおよそ1分間に150語です）。そして1語ずつ訳すのではなく、英語を英語のまま理解するくせをつけるようにします。こうして読み続けるうちに語感がついてきて、だんだんと英語が理解できるようになるのです。まずは、ラダーシリーズの中からあなたのレベルに合った本を選び、少しずつ英文に慣れ親しんでください。たくさんの本を手にとるうちに、英文書がすらすら読めるようになってくるはずです。

《本シリーズの特徴》
- 中学校レベルから中級者レベルまで5段階に分かれています。自分に合ったレベルからスタートしてください。
- クラシックから現代文学、ノンフィクション、ビジネスと幅広いジャンルを扱っています。あなたの興味に合わせてタイトルを選べます。
- 巻末のワードリストで、いつでもどこでも単語の意味を確認できます。レベル1、2では、文中の全ての単語が、レベル3以上は中学校レベル外の単語が掲載されています。
- カバーにヘッドホーンマークのついているタイトルは、オーディオ・サポートがあります。ウェブから購入／ダウンロードし、リスニング教材としても併用できます。

《使用語彙について》
レベル1：中学校で学習する単語約1000語

レベル2：レベル1の単語＋使用頻度の高い単語約300語

レベル3：レベル1の単語＋使用頻度の高い単語約600語

レベル4：レベル1の単語＋使用頻度の高い単語約1000語

レベル5：語彙制限なし

Contents

Foreword 3

Part 1 A Gifted Child 5

Part 2 Birth of a Startup 25

Part 3 World No. 1 49

Part 4 Bill Gates 2.0:
  The Philanthropist 79

Word List 98

読み始める前に

【読み進める上で知っておくと役に立つ単語】

- □ contract
- □ entrepreneur
- □ interface
- □ interpreter
- □ launch
- □ monopoly
- □ operating system
- □ optimist
- □ philanthropy
- □ predict

【ビル・ゲイツとマイクロソフトの変遷】

1955年	10月28日、シアトルでウィリアム・ゲイツ・シニアとマリー・ゲイツの間に生まれる。
1967年	私立レイクサイド校に入学。コンピューターに出会う。
1972年	ポール・アレンと共にトラフォデータ社を設立。
1973年	ハーバード大学に入学。スティーブ・バルマーと知り合う。
1975年	ハーバード大学を休学。MITS社のアルテア8800用プログラムを開発。マイクロソフトが設立される。
1979年	マイクロソフトの本社がニューメキシコからワシントンへ移る。
1980年	スティーブ・バルマーがマイクロソフトに入社。マイクロソフト、IBMのソフト提供契約に調印。
1983年	アレン、マイクロソフトを退社。
1985年	ウィンドウズ1.0が発売される。
1986年	マイクロソフトの株式を公開。日本マイクロソフトが設立される。
1988年	アップル社がマイクロソフトを著作権侵害で提訴。

Microsoft's Redmond campus

1990年	ウィンドウズ3.0を発売、大ヒットとなる。アレン、マイクロソフトに復帰。
1994年	メリンダ・フレンチと結婚。世界長者番付で世界一となり、以後たびたび首位を取る。
1995年	ウィンドウズ95を発売、世界的大ブームとなる。『The Road Ahead』を出版、ベストセラーになる。
1998年	ウィンドウズ98発売。
2000年	マイクロソフトのCEOを辞任。ビル&メリンダ・ゲイツ財団を創設。
2001年	ウィンドウズXP発売。
2004年	マイクロソフトの競争法違反に対して制裁金が科される。
2005年	タイム誌のパーソン・オブ・ザ・イヤーにメリンダと共に選出される。
2007年	ハーバード大学名誉学位号を授与される。
2008年	マイクロソフトの会長を辞任。
2016年	大統領自由勲章をメリンダと共に受章。

The Bill Gates Story

Tom Christian

Foreword

Technology or Business Genius?

Everybody has heard of Bill Gates. He is the father of the software industry, the world's richest person, a symbol of success. How did Gates achieve so much? It certainly wasn't by being nice to people. At Microsoft, Gates used to say "That's the stupidest thing I ever heard," whenever someone said something he disagreed with. His business competitors—whom he crushed without mercy—all hated him. His original business partner quit the company because Gates bullied him. People described him as "intense," "impatient" and "unpleasant."

Steve Jobs, another personal computer pioneer, did not think very highly of Gates. While he respected him for building the "first software company in the industry," he thought he was far better at making business deals than at making good products.

"Bill is unimaginative. He's never invented anything," Jobs said. "He just stole other people's ideas. That's why he's more comfortable now in philanthropy than technology."

Plenty of people agree with Steve Jobs. They think Bill Gates succeeded not because he was a technology genius but because he was very skilled at negotiating contracts and marketing.

Read this book and make up your own mind.

Part 1

A Gifted Child

A happy family

Bill Gates was born on October 28, 1955 in Seattle, Washington, into a rich upper-middle class family. His father, William H. Gates Senior, was a lawyer who later founded his own law firm. His mother, Mary M. Gates, came from a well-known family of Seattle bankers. She was originally a schoolteacher but started doing charity work after her marriage.

Bill was the middle child. He had a big sister, Kristianne, and a younger sister, Elizabeth. Life in the Gates family was fun, with plenty of intelligent conversation and games. Bill especially enjoyed playing board games like "Risk" and "Monopoly." ("Risk" is a military game; the goal is to conquer the world. "Monopoly" is a real-estate trading game; the goal is to get rich.) Playing these two games was good preparation for controlling the global software market and becoming the world's richest person!

PART 1 A GIFTED CHILD

Every summer the Gates family went to their summer house in the countryside near the Hood Canal in Washington. Bill was small and skinny with big glasses—a typical geek—but in fact he enjoyed playing tennis, swimming, water skiing, and other sports.

An unusually clever boy

Even when he was young, there were signs that Bill was much cleverer than his classmates. In fourth grade, when his science teacher asked him to write a five-page paper, he wrote one that was 30 pages long! He also won a competition to memorize a part of the Bible. The prize was dinner in the rotating restaurant at the top of Seattle's Space Needle, the 184-meter-tall observation tower that is the symbol of the city. Bill liked to read many books—and remembered most of what he read.

Bill knew that he was special. In fact, by the time he was eleven years old, he was becoming difficult to handle. He did not like grown-ups telling him what to do. One time, Bill was so rude to his mother that his father poured a glass of cold water over his head. Another time, when his mother asked him what he was doing, he replied sarcastically, "I'm thinking, mom. *You should try it some time.*"

William Senior and Mary were so worried by Bill's bad behavior that they took him to a therapist for help. The therapist encouraged Bill to read lots of books about psychology and to analyze himself. He told Bill's parents that their son was unusually clever and that it was probably impossible to control him. When Bill was thirteen, his parents decided to take him out of normal public school and put him in a private school, where he would get a better education.

Moving to a special school

Lakeside School was an expensive boys-only prep school in Seattle. The school was a traditional place in an old brick building. The boys had to wear a jacket and tie, go to chapel every morning, and call the teachers "master."

In 2005, Bill went back to Lakeside and made a speech explaining what made Lakeside so special. First, he said, the students and teachers really got to know one another, because the class sizes were small. As a result, the students took on difficult challenges because they liked and trusted their teachers. Bill's English teacher, for example, persuaded the shy little boy to try acting, and he took the lead part in the school play.

Second, the school was demanding. Bill got straight A's in chemistry; most schools would have been satisfied with that. But the teachers at Lakeside encouraged Bill to do more chemistry experiments (which he did not like doing) and not just learn all his chemistry from books.

Third, the education at Lakeside was practical. The things Bill learned there had a direct link to his career afterward. In fact, in his 2005 speech Bill said, "If there had been no Lakeside, there would have been no Microsoft. I can directly trace the founding of Microsoft back to my earliest days here."

First encounter with a computer

What was the connection between Bill's school and the founding of Microsoft?

Just a few months after Bill arrived at Lakeside, something happened that would decide the whole direction of his life. The school bought a Teletype terminal for a General Electric time-sharing minicomputer system. (In those days, a "minicomputer" was the size of a refrigerator and cost around $20,000! Because they cost so much, no school could buy one. Instead, they got a terminal and paid to access the computer via telephone. The terminal did not look like the PCs of today. It was just a keyboard and a printer; there was no screen.)

The Lakeside Mothers' Club then raised $3,000 by a rummage sale. They used the money to buy access to the computer—*which cost $40 per hour.* (Bill later explained that one reason he was so focused on making money was because computer time was so expensive in his boyhood.)

For Bill, it was love at first sight. He started

spending all his free time in the computer room. He even got the nickname "the computer guy" around the school.

The computer at Lakeside used the BASIC programming language. Gates quickly read the BASIC manual, mastered it and started making programs of his own. The first program he made was for playing tic-tac-toe. The computer was so slow that a game which took 30 seconds with a pencil and a piece of paper lasted the whole lunch hour!

None of the teachers at Lakeside understood computers. As a result, Bill had to teach himself. This is what made the experience so valuable. In the end, Bill even began teaching a computer class at the school.

Two teenage entrepreneurs

In the computer room, Bill met Paul Allen, a boy two years his senior. The two of them were quite different: Bill was shy and Paul was sociable. Bill could be rude (he often made fun of people less smart than himself), while

Paul was gentle. Bill always focused on one thing, but Paul liked to jump from one idea to another.

Even as teenagers, the two boys already dreamed of setting up their own company. In autumn 1968, when Bill was going into 8th grade, he, Paul and two other friends set up the Lakeside Programming Group and went into business. Their first job was for the Computer Center Corporation. In the evenings and at weekends, the boys would take the bus to the University of Washington and try to find bugs and "crash" the company's DEC computer. The boys were paid in free computer time. The man in charge of the DEC computer was Steve Russell who had created the world's first computer game, *Spacewar*, in 1962. Russell was amazed at how Bill could identify which programmer was responsible for which bugs in the program.

Bill and his friends lost access to the computer after they had successfully "debugged" the system. In the great tradition of Silicon Valley entrepreneurs, Bill hacked back into the system from school using a stolen password. When the Lakeside teachers found out what the boys were doing, they were forbidden to use the computer for quite a long time.

Gates in control

It was 1970. The next job the boys got was from a company called Information Systems Incorporated. They had to write a program to manage the company payroll. It was a difficult job because all the company's employees had different salaries and paid different taxes and social security contributions. But the pay was good: $18,000 of free computer time!

Paul and another boy in the group decided they could do the job without Bill. This was because the programming language for the job was COBOL, not BASIC, the programming language Bill was best at. Unfortunately for the two boys, the job turned out to be much harder than they thought. Halfway through, they asked Bill to help.

Bill decided to make sure that his friends

could never exclude him from any more jobs again. He got his father, who was a lawyer, to turn Lakeside Programming Group into a legal partnership with himself as president. In the end, it was Bill who took the biggest share of the free computing time!

Traf-O-Data and emulation

The work kept on coming. In fall 1971, Lakeside and a nearby girls' school joined together. The Lakeside administrators asked Bill and Paul (who was now at Washington University) to set up a scheduling program for the enlarged school. Bill set up the program so that he was in a history class where all the other students were girls! He also arranged for himself and his friends to have Tuesday afternoons free.

In 1972, Bill and Paul got a contract from the city of Seattle to analyze the flow of traffic in the city by counting the number of cars going down the road. The idea was to use a computer (instead of a person) to read the rolls of paper tape that got a hole punched in them every time a car drove by. Bill and Paul called the program they made to collect the data from the paper rolls Traf-O-Data (from "traffic" and "data").

There was nothing wrong with the software the boys made. The trouble was that when the representatives of the city of Seattle went to Bill's parents' house for a demonstration, the hardware did not work!

Although the project did not make much money for Bill and Paul, they did learn how to use a mainframe computer to "emulate," or copy, the way that Intel 8008 microprocessors worked. This knowledge was very useful later when they started Microsoft.

Leaving Lakeside

In Bill's final semester at Lakeside in spring 1973, he and Paul got a job with an electric power company to program the management system for the electrical grid. The headmaster allowed Bill to skip his whole final semester. Instead, he drove down to Portland and worked day and night in an underground bunker near the Columbia River doing coding.

Bill graduated that summer from Lakeside School with an SAT score of 1590 out of 1600. He had applied to three Ivy League colleges, Harvard, Yale and Princeton. He decided to go to Harvard.

Harvard life

Bill went to Harvard in fall 1973. He shared his dorm room with a boy from a poor Jewish refugee family from Montreal and a black boy from Tennessee. Bill's two roommates were amazed to see him filling out tax forms for all the money he had earned through his programming work.

Bill was a pre-law major, but he decided that it would be "cool" to be lazy and not to go to class. Then he started taking some of most difficult mathematics and computer courses, even though he was not signed up for them.

Bill behaved with his usual intensity at Harvard. He used to study for 36 hours, sleep for

10 hours, eat some junk food and then go right back to studying. When he was concentrating, he often rocked back and forth. When it was time to relax, Bill would play *Pong*, the video game version of table tennis, or *Spacewar*, the game created by Steve Russell at Computer Center Corporation. He also took up poker, sometimes winning or losing $1,000 in a night!

Meeting Steve Ballmer

In one of his economics classes, Bill met someone called Steve Ballmer. The two young men were opposites: Bill didn't take part in campus activities, while Ballmer was involved in everything. Bill was small and shy, while Ballmer was big, loud and friendly. Ballmer was manager of the football team, advertising manager for the Harvard newspaper, and publisher of the Harvard literary magazine. Both young men were intense and smart. They liked to have long and loud discussions and then go and see movies like *Singing in the Rain* and *A Clockwork Orange* to relax. Ballmer was to play an important part in Microsoft in the future.

New chips and *Popular Electronics*

In spring 1974, Intel released its new 8080 microprocessor. The 8080 was *10 times more powerful* than the 8008 from two years before, but only around *half the price*. Computing power was getting cheaper and faster all the time.

Bill and Paul thought that with these Intel chips it would be possible to make small computers cheap enough for ordinary people to buy. The two boys sent letters from Gates' dorm room to the big computer companies offering to write a new version of BASIC for the Intel 8080. They got no replies.

In the summer of 1974, Gates persuaded Paul to drop out of Washington University, get a job with Honeywell and move to Boston. (Back then, Boston was a major computing center. It was home to companies like Digital Equipment Corp., Wang Laboratories and

Part 1 A Gifted Child

Data General Corp.)

In December 1974, Paul Allen was looking through the magazines in a book shop in Harvard Square when he noticed the latest edition of *Popular Electronics*. There was a picture of the Altair, the world's first home microcomputer, on its front cover. Paul paid 75 cents for the magazine and ran over to Bill's dorm room. "Hey, Bill," said Paul, "the personal computer revolution is happening without us!"

The Altair

Compared to personal computers now, the Altair was a cheap and simple piece of equipment. It cost just $397 and came as a kit, meaning that you had to assemble it yourself. It had no monitor, no keyboard and no mouse. Nor did it have a programming language or an operating system. It had just 4 kB of memory—several million times less memory than a modern smartphone! You entered data using 16 switches and the computer gave results via 16 LED lights. "You could get the sixteen little lights on the front panel to blink on and off," Bill later said. "But that was about all."

Contacting MITS

The Intel 8080 microprocessor in the Altair needed an "interpreter" for the BASIC programming language before it could understand instructions. An interpreter, in other words, would made it possible for other people to write programs for the Altair. Bill and Paul decided that they would try to make one.

The company which made the Altair was called Micro Instrumentation and Telemetry Systems, or MITS. It was based 2,300 kilometers away in Albuquerque, New Mexico. The founder, Ed Roberts, started manufacturing electronic calculator kits in 1971 before moving into computer kits.

Bill called Roberts. "We've nearly finished a BASIC language interpreter for the Altair," he said. "We'd like to show it to you." (Bill was lying. He and Paul had not yet started!)

Many other people had called Roberts to say

the same thing. He gave Bill the same reply he gave everyone else: "The first person to walk through my door in Albuquerque with a finished product will get the contract."

Building a BASIC interpreter

For the next two months, Bill and Paul worked like crazy writing software. Since they did not have an Altair, they had to do the same thing they had done with the Traf-O-Data project: use "emulation" techniques to make an Altair simulator on the Harvard mainframe. While Paul did that, Bill wrote out the BASIC interpreter code. Eventually, they got so busy that they hired a third person, Monte Davidoff.

Bill was supposed to be preparing for exams. Instead, he and his two friends worked day and night. It was extremely difficult to make the program small enough to fit into the computer's tiny memory, but by the end of February 1975 it was ready.

"Sometimes I rock back and forth or pace when I'm thinking, because it helps me focus on a single idea," Bill later wrote. "I did a lot of rocking and pacing in my dorm room the winter of 1975. Paul and I didn't sleep much and lost track of night and day. I slept at my desk or on the floor. Some days I didn't eat or see anyone."

Success in New Mexico

Paul, who was twenty-two and had a beard, looked older than Gates. That's why he flew down to Albuquerque to demonstrate their software to Ed Roberts at MITS. Even so, Roberts was quite surprised at how young Paul was—and even more surprised when he had to pay for Paul's hotel room, because he didn't have enough money!

For the demonstration, Paul asked the computer a simple question: "PRINT 2+2." The Altair printed "4." Roberts, whose company was heavily in debt, got very excited. "Oh my God!" he shouted, thinking that now he had the chance to make some money. "It printed four!"

PART 1 A GIFTED CHILD

Roberts agreed to license Bill and Paul's BASIC interpreter for the Altair. When Paul got back to Cambridge, the boys went out to celebrate. Gates was still under the legal drinking age so he had a Shirley Temple (ginger ale with cherry juice).

Soon after, Roberts offered Paul the job of software director. Paul gave up his job at Honeywell and moved to Albuquerque to work at MITS. Bill stayed at Harvard to finish his second year, but he was in trouble with the university authorities. They were unhappy because he had let Paul use the university mainframe computer. The computer was funded by the Defense Advanced Research Projects Agency (DARPA), which is part of the government. Non-students were not allowed to use it.

A good contract

In the summer of 1975, Bill flew down to Albuquerque to join Paul. As the boys did not have a lot of money, they lived in a motel full of prostitutes before moving to a cheap furnished apartment. Bill quickly made a written contract with MITS.

The contract was for a period of 10 years and Bill and Paul got from $30 to $60 per copy of software sold. (Different Altair computers had slightly different software.) Most importantly, Bill and Paul owned the software, not MITS. MITS also promised to make its "best efforts" to license the software to other computer makers.

The contract was to Bill's advantage. He was to make a similar one with IBM five years later.

Part 2

Birth of a Startup

The Altair 8810: the first commercially successful personal computer

The birth of "Micro-Soft"

Bill and Paul needed a name for their new company. They thought about "Gates and Allen," but felt that it sounded like a law firm. Eventually they chose Micro-Soft, because their business was making *soft*ware for *micro*-computers. (By the end of 1976, the name was Microsoft, with no hyphen.)

At the beginning, there were four people in Micro-Soft: Bill Gates, Paul Allen, Monte Davidoff from Harvard, and Chris Larson, a friend from Lakeside. To pay for setting up the firm, they used money from Paul's salary at Honeywell and Bill's winnings from playing poker at Harvard.

When they set up the company, Bill and Paul had to decide how to divide up the company. As usual, Bill negotiated a good deal for himself. He gave himself the biggest share— 64% of the company versus just 36% for Paul!

Bill said this was "fair" because Allen was getting $30,000 a year from MITS as software director. It was also because Bill's father was a lawyer. Contracts were in Bill's blood.

Work hard, play hard

The four young men worked hard and played hard in typical Silicon Valley style. Bill often had very fierce arguments with Ed Roberts, the boss of MITS, and the two men would shout at one another. When they wanted to relax after programming until late at night, Paul played along with Jimi Hendrix and Aerosmith on his guitar, while Bill drove his car at high speed in the desert. Because they worked so intensively, they could sell their software more cheaply than their competitors.

Although Bill took a leave of absence from Harvard for the fall semester of 1975, he did complete the spring and fall semesters of 1976. After that he dropped out completely. He did promise his father that he would go back and finish his degree one day. In 2007, when

Harvard awarded Bill an honorary doctorate, he made a speech. "I've been waiting more than thirty years to say this," he said. "Dad, I told you I'd come back and get my degree."

Problems with piracy

By the end of 1975, MITS was selling 1,000 Altairs every month. Ed Roberts promoted the Altair by driving around California and other states and visiting the local computer clubs. The problem for Microsoft was that only about one person out of ten who bought Altair hardware was actually paying for the software. People then were not accustomed to the idea of paying for software; most of them got free copies from friends. Since many of the early users of microcomputers belonged to clubs, it was very easy for them to share copied software.

In February 1976, Bill tried to fight back by publishing his "Open Letter to Hobbyists" in the Homebrew Computer Club Newsletter. (The Homebrew Computer Club was based in Silicon Valley. Steve Wozniak, an Apple co-founder, was a member.)

In the letter, Bill explained that making good quality software costs time and money. The users of Altair BASIC who used free copies were "stealing" software. Was it fair to pay for hardware and not to pay for software? Stealing software will stop good software being made, because no one wants to work for free. Bill suggested that the computer clubs should expel any member who was selling copied software. Finally, he asked anyone who was using an unpaid-for copy of his software to send him a letter with money in it.

Bill received 300 letters in response. Only five of them contained any money; most of them just said rude things. "I got a lot of shit," commented Gates. Ironically, though, piracy may have helped Microsoft BASIC to spread widely and become the standard. (By 1977, Apple and Commodore computers were also using Microsoft software.)

Leaving New Mexico

On January 1, 1979, Bill moved Microsoft from Albuquerque to the suburbs of Seattle. This was for several reasons: Firstly, Seattle was Bill's home town; secondly, there was more computing talent in Washington State than in remote New Mexico; and thirdly, Ed Roberts had sold MITS to a Californian company in 1977, so it was no longer necessary for Microsoft to be in New Mexico.

After moving to Seattle, Microsoft was ready to embark on the second chapter of its story. It was going to progress from making programming languages to the next stage, creating operating systems and then creating applications.

Bringing Ballmer on board

Microsoft was getting bigger every year and Bill knew that he needed help running the business. He decided that Steve Ballmer, his friend from Harvard, was the right man for the job.

Part 2 Birth of a Startup

After graduating in 1977, Ballmer had worked at consumer goods company P&G for a couple of years. In 1979, he enrolled on an MBA course at Stanford.

Bill really wanted Ballmer, but Ballmer was not sure if it was a good idea to join his friend's small startup. Bill invited Ballmer to Seattle, gave him a tour of the city and took him out to dinner with his parents. He also offered him an 8% share of the company to persuade him to join. Stock in Microsoft ended up making Ballmer one of the 30 richest people in the world!

Ballmer joined Microsoft on June 11, 1980. He and Bill argued quite soon afterward. Bill, who ran the young company very conservatively, was shocked when Ballmer proposed hiring 50 more people immediately. (There were only 30 people in the company at the time!) Finally, Bill agreed to Ballmer's suggestion. Later, Bill said that hiring Ballmer was "one of the two best business decisions he ever took in his life, along with going into business with Paul Allen in the first place."

Partnering with "Big Blue"

Ballmer was right to hire more people. Microsoft was about to start expanding faster than anyone could imagine. On July 21, about five weeks after Ballmer joined, Bill got a call from IBM. The next day Jack Sams, an IBM engineer, flew to Seattle.

At this time, IBM was the dominant mainframe computer manufacturer with an 80% market share. It employed 350,000 people and generated roughly $30 billion in revenues per year. Nonetheless, the company had some problems. It was the market leader for mainframes (the biggest computers), but other companies like Digital Equipment Corporation (DEC) and Wang Laboratories were outperforming it in the market for minicomputers (the second biggest computers).

IBM could see that microcomputers were about to become very popular. It did not want to miss out on this new market category. IBM wanted to launch a personal computer, or PC, within one year. IBM was used to making big machines for large corporations. Since nobody at IBM had the know-how to make cheap, small machines for ordinary consumers, they decided to look outside for help, getting their microprocessors from Intel and their operating system (OS) from Microsoft.

The origins of PC-DOS

Jack Sams was in charge of developing software for the IBM-PC. When he asked Microsoft if they could provide an operating system, Bill told him that Microsoft did not actually make an OS itself. Instead, Bill sent the IBM team to a company called Digital Research run by his old friend Gary Kildall. Kildall had developed an OS called CP/M.

Like a lot of computer entrepreneurs, Gary was a bit of a free spirit. Instead of meeting with the boring men in suits from IBM, he went flying in his airplane and sent his wife to the meeting. She did not like the way they tried to make her sign a non-disclosure agreement and told them to go away.

Sams went back to Microsoft. Could they help him? This is when Bill realized that the best thing would be for Microsoft to make IBM's OS itself. Paul Allen knew Tim Paterson, a software engineer at Seattle Computer Products. Paterson had developed an operating system called 86-DOS. In December 1980, Microsoft paid $25,000 for a non-exclusive license to 86-DOS. Then they hired Paterson to modify 86-DOS for the IBM-PC and then, Microsoft bought 100% of 86-DOS for another $50,000. (Bill did not tell Seattle Computer Products about Microsoft's deal with IBM. If they had known about it, they would never have sold him their operating system at such a cheap price.) The IBM version of 86-DOS was called PC-DOS.

The art of the deal

IBM paid Microsoft $186,000 for PC-DOS. This was not a lot of money. However, IBM only got a non-exclusive license to PC-DOS, leaving Microsoft free to license the OS to other computer companies (as MS-DOS). Microsoft also kept complete control of the source code.

With the computer hardware, IBM had chosen an "open-architecture approach." They published the specs of their machine, enabling other computer makers to make "clones" and copy it. Bill was expecting other manufacturers to do just that. That's why he negotiated a contract that allowed Microsoft to make software for IBM clones too.

IBM unveiled their new PC on August 12, 1981 at a big ceremony at the Waldorf Astoria Hotel in New York. No one from Microsoft was invited. As far as IBM was concerned, Microsoft was just a lowly supplier.

Cheap by design

The first IBM-PC actually shipped with three operating system options. There was Microsoft's PC-DOS, Digital Research's CP/M-86 and the USCD Pascal p-System. The prices were very different—PC-DOS cost $60, CP/M $175 and Pascal $450.

Selling cheap was a strategic decision. "Microsoft licensed the software at extremely low prices. It was our belief that money could be made betting on volume," Bill later explained. He did not want to make money directly from IBM, but by licensing the same OS to all the other computer companies that started making IBM-compatible machines. This led to Microsoft BASIC becoming the industry standard.

Dawn of the PC age

The launch of the IBM-PC triggered the first personal computer revolution. Now it was not just hobbyists who wanted a personal computer—everybody wanted one. By January 1983, the IBM-PC was being sold globally. Somebody, somewhere in the world bought an IBM-PC every minute of every business day.

Personal computers became so popular, that *Time* magazine named the PC as the "Machine of the Year" for 1982 (instead of its normal "Man of the Year"). Americans, *Time* said, had shifted their love of automobiles and then televisions to the personal computer.

Other companies sensed an opportunity. By the mid-1980s, new firms like Compaq, Dell and Hewlett Packard were making IBM-compatible personal computers that ran MS-DOS. Software developers also started creating applications for PCs such as Lotus 1-2-3.

The combination of good hardware and good software turned the IBM-PC and its clones into the global standard. Three years after the IBM-PC debuted, all other competing standards, except for Apple II and Macintosh, had disappeared.

Paul Allen gets sick

One sad thing happened amid all this success. In late 1982, Paul Allen, Bill's co-founder, discovered that he had cancer. He had to take time off work for treatment. When he came back to the office, he overheard Bill talking to Ballmer about how they could cut his share in the company. Paul was shocked. He was dangerously sick, and all his old friend and colleague could think about was money!

Paul decided that he no longer wanted to work with either Bill or Ballmer, and he quit the company in 1983. Bill offered to buy Paul's shares for $5.00 each, but when Paul asked for $10.00, he refused to pay. Paul's Microsoft shares later became enormously valuable ($23 billion in 2017). That's why Paul Allen is sometimes called "the accidental billionaire."

Xerox PARC and the GUI

Although the IBM-PC was cheaper and easier to use than the mainframes and minicomputers of the 1980s, the interface was far more complicated than the computers we use today. The early IBM-PCs were just green text and numbers on a black screen. To get the computer to do anything, you had to type in commands.

Computers now are much easier to use. That's because they have a graphical user interface (GUI) with a desktop with folders, overlapping documents and pull-down menus which you control with a mouse. The graphical user interface was developed by researchers at Xerox Palo Alto Research Center (Xerox PARC).

Xerox produced the world's first personal computer with a graphical user interface in 1981. Known as the Xerox Star, it cost a whopping $16,500. Apple's Lisa, the second computer with a GUI which came out in 1983, was not much cheaper. It cost $9,995.

Working with Steve Jobs

Steve Jobs, the Apple co-founder, made it his mission to develop the first *affordable* personal computer with a GUI. This was the Apple Macintosh. When it was released in January 1984, it cost just $2,495, one quarter of the Apple Lisa, and one sixth of the Xerox Star. The launch of the Macintosh was a milestone: thanks to the GUI, personal computers really were personal and easy to use.

In August 1981, Steve Jobs, asked Microsoft to develop graphical software applications for Apple's Macintosh computers. (These products later became Excel and Word.) Bill hired Charles Simonyi, an engineer from Xerox PARC, as product development manager.

"Working with Steve, who led the Apple team, was great fun," Gates later wrote. "Steve has an amazing intuition for engineering and design as well as an ability to motivate people that is world class."

Steve Jobs and Bill Gates in 2007
Joi Ito

Gates bets big on GUI

Microsoft had complete access to Apple's OS technology while it was building software for the Apple Macintosh. Steve Jobs was very worried. What if Bill Gates tried to copy his graphical user interface and put it in IBM-PCs? To prevent this, Jobs made Microsoft sign a contract. In the contract, Microsoft promised not to make any software with a mouse or a GUI until the end of 1983, one year after the planned launch of the Macintosh. (The Macintosh actually launched more than one year late.)

Bill could see that the GUI was the future of personal computing. In November 1982 at COMDEX, the big computer exhibition Las Vegas, VisiCorp demonstrated Visi On, its graphical user OS for IBM-compatible PCs. *Microsoft needed to make its own operating system with a graphical user interface, or it would be left behind!*

In June 1983, Bill wrote a memo outlining Microsoft's future.

Xerox PARC's vision is the future of Microsoft. Microsoft believes in mouse and graphics as invaluable to the man-machine interface. We will bet on that belief by focusing new development on two new environments with mouse and graphics, Macintosh and Windows.

That same month, Bill hired Steve McGregor, another young engineer from Xerox PARC. McGregor's job was to create Windows, a GUI-based operating system for IBM-PCs. While McGregor was developing the new system, Bill often came to look at his work. If he did not like it, he would say, "Why isn't this more like the Mac? Make it more like the Mac."

Windows comes out

In November 1983, Bill held a press conference at the New York Palace Hotel. He announced that Microsoft was developing Windows, a new operating system for IBM-PCs and

IBM-compatible PCs.

Windows 1.0 came out two years later in November 1985. The reviews were rather negative: they described the system as "memory hungry" and "slow." Some people also think that Windows 1.0 was the original "vaporware." ("Vaporware" is a product that is announced a long time before it actually comes out to stop customers buying another product instead.)

Jobs was furiously angry when Windows came out. He summoned Bill to Apple's office in Cupertino. "I trusted you and now you're stealing from us," Jobs shouted at him. "Well, Steve," Bill replied calmly. "I think there's more than one way of looking at it. I think it's more like we both had this rich neighbor named Xerox and I broke into his house to steal the TV set and found out that you had already stolen it."

This argument did not convince Jobs. Apple launched a lawsuit against Microsoft for stealing the idea of a graphical user interface. (Apple lost).

IBM's fatal mistake

In 1984, IBM earned $6.6 billion, a new record for the biggest annual profit of any company ever. The company also launched its second-generation personal computer, the PC/AT, which captured 70% of the business PC market inside one year.

At the same time, however, IBM was getting nervous. It did not like being completely dependent on Microsoft for its software. It was also worried that as personal computers got more powerful, they would destroy its existing business in mainframes and minicomputers.

In August 1985, IBM started working with Microsoft to develop OS/2, a next-generation operating system. IBM wanted an operating system that could "multitask" (run multiple programs at the same time).

IBM decided to use the same systems applications architecture for OS/2 that it used in its mainframes and minicomputers. They wanted to keep all IBM customers, whether of IBM-PCs, minicomputers or mainframes, locked into IBM software.

IBM was also worried about the success that companies like Compaq, Dell and Hewlett Packard were having selling IBM-compatible PCs. The company decided to create its own new hardware so that it could charge the other computer manufacturers a license fee.

Unfortunately, having an operating system that was compatible with old mainframes made the new IBM personal computers just as slow and heavy as mainframes. OS/2, for example, took 3 minutes to boot (be ready to use after switching on the computer).

In April 1987, IBM unveiled OS/2 and the PS/2, its "clone-killer" computer. The plan was for IBM's OS/2 to take the top end of the market (and become the world's main operating system), while Microsoft's Windows took the low end of the market and a smaller market share.

Things did not go according to plan. Customers found IBMs new software difficult to use (and it didn't work on most people's computers anyway). Everyone preferred Windows because it was fast and had memory and graphics. "The worse OS/2 looked, the better Windows seemed," Bill commented later.

Getting behind Windows

Although Windows went on to become one of the world's most famous brand names, neither Bill nor Steve Ballmer gave the product much support in the first few years of its life. The only reason that Windows 3.0, which came out in May 1990, was such a success was because a couple of engineers secretly "hacked" it into protected mode. ("Protected mode" means having multitasking capabilities and more memory for each application.)

In fact, Bill and Ballmer were planning to stop developing Windows after Windows 3.0. They were astonished when Windows 3.0 became a huge hit.

Why was Windows 3.0 so popular? For three reasons: First, the graphical user interface was much better than before. Second, when Windows came out, Windows versions of Excel,

Word and PowerPoint were also available, while there were no applications ready for OS/2 because IBM was so slow and bureaucratic. If you wanted to do spreadsheets, word-processing or presentations, Windows was the better choice. And third, all the old DOS applications also worked on Windows 3.0.

Windows 3.0 sold 4 million copies in one year. Everyone began to see the appeal of the graphical user interface. The success of Windows made Microsoft's applications popular. By 1995 Microsoft had a 60% share of the word-processing and spreadsheet market.

Many people thought that this success was the result of Bill's strategy. They were sure that Bill tricked IBM by *pretending* to work hard on developing OS/2 with them when he was secretly developing Windows as an OS/2 killer all the time. In fact, the whole thing was just a lucky accident. Windows 3.0 had to sell one million copies before Gates realized that his software was more popular than IBM's OS/2. In 1991, Microsoft and IBM officially split up and stopped joint development of OS/2.

Part 3

World No. 1

Bill and Melinda Gates
Kjetil Ree

A wild young man

In March 1986, Bill took Microsoft public. The company was listed on the NASDAQ Exchange at $21 per share. At the age of just 31, Bill, who owned 45% of the company, was worth $350 million. By 1987, as the stock price kept rising, he was the world's youngest billionaire.

In the 1980s, while he was still a bachelor, Gates was quite wild. He used to hold parties at his house with girls hired from local nightclubs swimming naked in his pool. He also had a reputation for trying to sleep with female journalists who came to interview him about his company.

He was not a very easy person to go out with. One of his girlfriends from the 1980s said that it was difficult to have a relationship with a man who was proud of having a "turnaround time" of seven hours. (Bill meant that he was never away from Microsoft for more than seven hours per day. In other words, he spent 17 hours out of 24 at work!)

Meeting Melinda

In 1987, Bill went to New York for a trade-fair dinner. Sitting beside him was 28-year-old Melinda French, a young woman from Dallas, Texas, who had joined Microsoft four months earlier after an internship at IBM. Melinda had an undergraduate degree in computer science and an MBA from Duke University.

A few weeks later, Bill met her in the company carpark and asked her on a date. "Can we go out *two weeks from this coming Saturday*?" Bill said. Melinda said no. She didn't like being asked on a date as if she were being asked to a business meeting. It was all too well-planned, not spontaneous enough.

Bill went away, then called her an hour later "Is this spontaneous enough for you?" he asked. "Why don't we go out tonight?" As it was quite late, none of the restaurants in

Seattle were open, so they just went to Bill's house and talked.

Over the years, Melinda advanced inside the company. She started managing multimedia products like *Encarta*, the CD-Rom encyclopedia, Expedia, the travel website, and Microsoft Publishing, a desktop publishing application.

In March 1993, Bill proposed to Melinda. She said yes and they then got on a plane and flew 2,600 kilometers to Omaha. There they went to Borsheim's, the jewelry store owned by Bill's friend the billionaire investor Warren Buffett, and bought an engagement ring.

That August, Bill and Melinda went to Africa for a 3-week vacation. "Melinda and I went to Africa to see the wildlife, and we were startled by the poverty," Gates said. "It blew our minds that millions of children were dying from diarrhea, pneumonia, and malaria. Kids in rich countries don't die from these things. The children in Africa were dying because they were poor. To us, it was the most unjust thing in the world. It's inspired our work ever since."

This was the first sign that perhaps one day

Bill would move beyond Microsoft and get into philanthropy.

A very private ceremony

With his wealth, Bill was now one of the most famous people in the world. It was going to be difficult to keep photographers away from his wedding. Bill decided that the best way to keep things private was to hold the ceremony on Lanai, a small private island in Hawaii. Because the island was privately owned, it was easier to control visitors.

Lanai had once been the property of James Dole, the "Pineapple King." Dole had turned it into the world's biggest pineapple plantation. The island now belonged to Castle and Cooke Properties, a Dole subsidiary. Castle and Cooke started developing the island for tourists in the early 1990s, and the Manele Bay Hotel (now Four Seasons Resort Lanai) had opened in 1991.

Bill booked all the available rooms at the

hotel to stop journalists staying there. He also hired all the helicopters on the nearby island of Maui to stop photographers taking pictures from the air. To mislead the media, Bill and Melinda told people they were going to be married on February 14, Valentine's day, 1994.

In fact, the wedding took place on January 1, 1994. Many famous guests came. They included Microsoft co-founder Paul Allen; billionaire investor Warren Buffett; and Katherine Graham, owner of The Washington Post. Steve Ballmer was Bill's best man.

The ceremony was held at sunset on the 12th hole of the hotel golf course. At the party, Willie Nelson, Melinda's favorite singer, provided the entertainment. Bill and Melinda then flew on a private jet to Fiji for their honeymoon.

One wedding and a funeral

Sadly, less than six months after the wedding, Bill's mother Mary died from breast cancer. She was only 64 years old. Around 1,000 people came to her funeral. Gates made a speech. In it, he talked about how proud he was of his mother and mentioned that she had been very helpful in persuading Steve Ballmer to join Microsoft back in 1980.

The headline of Mary's obituary in the *New York Times* was: "Mary Gates, 64; Helped Her Son Start Microsoft." But did Mary really play a big part in Microsoft's early success? In 1980, Mary was on the board of a charity called United Way of America. One other board member was John R. Opel, the chairman of IBM. According to the *New York Times*, Mary mentioned her son's little software company to the IBM chairman, and a few weeks later IBM hired Microsoft to develop the operating system for the IBM-PC. Did the IBM chairman encourage his executives to choose Microsoft? Nobody knows.

Mary Gates wrote a letter to Bill and Melinda the day before their wedding. "From those to whom much is given, much is expected," she said. Certainly, as Bill got older, he got more involved in working for the community like his mother. Just a few months after his mother died, Gates gave about $100 million to the William H. Gates Foundation, a charity which his father ran.

Bill's dream house

In 1988, Bill bought five acres of land just outside Seattle overlooking Lake Washington and the Olympic Mountains. Here he started building a house worthy of the world's software king. The house took seven years to build and cost $63 million. It is called Xanadu 2.0 after Xanadu, the mansion of the millionaire Charles Foster Kane in the 1941 movie *Citizen Kane*.

The house has all sorts of luxurious features: exterior walls of 500-year-old wood; a 20-meter pool with an underwater music system; a trampoline room with a 6-meter ceiling; a reception room with space for 100 people; a 20-seat home theater; a racquetball court; a 200-square-meter library containing the $30.8 million *Codex Leicester*, the only Leonardo da Vinci manuscript in private hands; a beach with sand imported from the Caribbean; a 30-meter pier for water-skiing...

The estate actually contains two houses, the main house and a smaller guest house. Work started on the guest house in 1990 and on the main house in 1992. Bill wanted the main house to be very high tech, so he tested all the technology in the guest house first. There is a remote control to manage the lighting, heating, air-conditioning, music, video and security. Bill experimented with audio speakers that came out of the roof, but finally decided they were "too James Bond-like."

Visitors to the main house are given an electronic pin to clip to their clothes. This pin contains information on their preferences for music, art, lighting, and so on. Twenty-four video monitors in the reception area display digital art work to match their tastes. As visitors move around the house, sensors switch the lights on and off, while music and movies follow then from room to room.

There is a 1.5-meter gap between the walls

of each room. This space is full cables, computers, TV monitors and other electronic equipment.

Of course, technology does not always work the way it is supposed to. According to one story, the first night that Bill spent in the house he could not turn off the TV in the bedroom. In the end, he just had to cover it with a blanket!

Windows conquers the world

After the launch of Windows 3.0 in May 1990, Windows 3.1 came out in April 1992 and Windows 93 in June 1993. The biggest product launch, however, was for Windows 95, which came out on August 24, 1995. By this stage, 140 million people around the world were using either Windows or DOS.

There was a huge advertising campaign for Windows 95. Microsoft spent around $300 million directly promoting the operating system; electronics shops and computer makers spent another $700 million. Because

PART 3 WORLD NO. 1

of Windows 95's new "Start" button, the key word of the advertising was "start." Microsoft spent $3 million to buy the rights to use the Rolling Stones' song *Start Me Up*. The company also produced a Windows 95 video guide featuring Jennifer Aniston (Brad Pitt's first wife) and Matthew Perry, two stars from the hit TV comedy *Friends*.

Two thousand guests—including 500 journalists—came to the August 24 launch event at Microsoft's Seattle campus. There were big tents, a Ferris wheel and a stage where Jay Leno, a TV comedian, hosted an all-day event. "Windows 95 is so easy that even a talk show host can figure it out," Bill joked.

The promotion was both a nationwide and a worldwide effort. The Empire State Building in New York was lit up in the colors of Windows 95. In London, *The Times* newspaper was given away free for one day with a special section all about Windows 95.

In a practice that later became common with products like the Harry Potter books and the Apple iPhone, shops around the world opened at midnight so people could buy the software as early as possible. The first person in the world to buy Windows 95 was a business student in Auckland, New Zealand.

The campaign clearly worked: Windows 95 sold 19 million copies in just four months.

Bill Gates: Long-sighted visionary

In 1993, Bill started work on a book on the future of computers. He wrote it with Nathan Myhrvold, Microsoft's in-house technology guru. As usual, Bill negotiated a fantastic deal. Penguin Group, the publisher, promised to print 500,000 copies and spend $125,000 on marketing. They also paid Bill a $2.5 million advance. (The book's profits were given to a foundation to encourage computer use in schools.) The title of the book was *The Road Ahead*. The photo on the front cover, taken by Annie Leibovitz, shows Bill standing on an empty road.

The Road Ahead came out in November 1995. It was No. 1 on the *New York Times* bestseller list for two months. Generally, people felt that the book sold well because Bill was the most famous person in the world rather than because it was a good book.

The *New York Times* review said that the book was "designed mainly to advance the interests of the Microsoft Corporation," and it certainly mentioned quite a few Microsoft products like the *Encarta* encyclopedia and the *Flight Simulator* game. Many reviewers were surprised at how little attention Bill paid to the Internet. (In fact, Gates later revised the book, adding much more content about the Internet.)

The Road Ahead: Part I

The Road Ahead begins with the story of how Bill first encountered computers at school; it then turns into a history of the first 20 years of Microsoft.

Bill tries to explain his company's success as being the result of other companies' mistakes. Other computer makers, he says, failed to notice the "next industry turn." For example,

IBM missed the switch from mainframes to minicomputers *and* the switch from minicomputers to personal computers. Meanwhile, Digital Equipment Corp. (DEC) and Wang Laboratories, the minicomputer leaders, missed the switchover from minicomputers to personal computers.

Bill suggests that it was IBM's fault that it lost out to Microsoft. "As PCs became more powerful, to avoid having them cannibalize its higher-end products, IBM held back on PC development. But it could not "control" the market, as it did with mainframes and minicomputers."

The lesson that Bill draws from other companies' failure is that "Death can come swiftly to a market leader."

The book compares the personal computer revolution to the effect of the printing press. Bill points out that the number of books in the world rose from 30,000 in 1450 to one million by 1500 after Johannes Gutenberg invented printing. This part of the book aimed to present Gates as a great "man of destiny" who had become very successful partly through big trends and partly through other people's mistakes.

The Road Ahead: Part II

The second part of the book—the part of the book that Bill wrote with futurologist Nathan Myhrvold—is all about the "information superhighway." ("Information superhighway" is an outdated expression that refers to the coming together of TV content and computers.)

This section does a brilliant job of predicting the technology we have now. For example, it talks about "pocket-sized computers" that will "display and manage schedules and let you read and send electronic mail and faxes, monitor weather and stock reports and play games." That sounds a lot like the iPhone. It also predicts PCs and TVs with voice recognition. That sounds a lot like Apple's Siri.

The book correctly predicts the future of gaming with massively multiplayer online games (MMOGs); the future of education with massive open online courses (MOOCs); and the future of work with people "collaborating easily from virtually anywhere."

When *The Road Ahead* came out in 1995, the e-commerce company Amazon.com was just one year old. Nevertheless, Bill and Myhrvold correctly forecast that "delivering goods over the highway will become a big business." They also warn that newspapers will start experiencing financial problems when classified ads move online. That is exactly what happened.

Foreseeing disruption

In fact, Bill and Myhrvold predict that the "information highway" will cause such dramatic change that people will start to feel worried. "Industry after industry will be changed and change is unsettling. There will be dislocations. However, overall society will benefit from these changes. Entire professions and industries will fade. But new ones will flourish," they say, taking an optimistic point of view.

The book does point out some negative effects technology will have on society. If people can get all the entertainment they need from the "information superhighway," they will live increasingly lonely lives, spending all their time on the computer instead of with other people. At the same time, with computers and security cameras keeping track of everyone, privacy and computer security will become serious problems. Unfortunately, Bill and Myhrvold were right about that too!

Looking too far ahead?

Bill and his co-writer did a fantastic job of predicting the world we live in now—the world of broadband internet with YouTube, Netflix, TED talks, Skype, Amazon Prime and WikiLeaks.

Unfortunately, in the mid-1990s when *The Road Ahead* came out, this broadband world was still 10 years or more away. Some critics complained that Myhrvold was *too much* of a futurist. The Internet of 1995—fast enough for e-mail and web browsing but too slow for movies, gaming or teleconferencing—was just too boring for Myhrvold, so he ignored it.

Myhrvold was so excited by the broadband "information highway" of the future that Microsoft almost missed the narrow-band Internet which was right in front of their noses. In fact it was Netscape, a much younger and smaller company, that was the first to see the Internet's potential.

The rise of Netscape

On April 4, 1994, Jim Clark, a 50-year-old millionaire entrepreneur, and Marc Andreesen, a 22-year-old programmer, set up a company called Netscape Communications. Andreesen had recently graduated in computer science from the University of Illinois. At Illinois, Andreesen worked at the National Center for Supercomputing Applications (NCSA). Impressed by the way that university scientists were using the World Wide Web to share information, Andreesen had teamed up with another student, Eric Bina, to create Mosaic, the world's first web browser, to help them.

On October 13, 1994, Netscape posted a test version of its Navigator browser on the Internet. (The test version was free; starting in 1995 you had to pay for it.) There were only 16 million Internet users in 1994, but the number started to double every year. Over 5 million copies of Netscape Navigator were downloaded within six months. In August 1995, Netscape was listed on the Nasdaq stock exchange in New York. There was huge demand and the market valued the company—little more than one year old and with tiny revenues—at $3 billion dollars. Suddenly no one cared about Windows 95 anymore. The big news now was Netscape and the Internet.

"Getting" the Internet

Compared to Netscape, Microsoft was slow to "get" the Internet. Bill was suspicious, because he was worried about security. With the Internet, people could steal and publish Microsoft's code. (This had happened with Apple.) In addition, the Internet was free and Bill was always focused on making money. When someone first suggested that Microsoft should give away its browser for nothing like Netscape, Bill yelled, "Are you a communist?"

Bill used to take "Think Weeks," when he went away for a week to think deeply about the long-term direction of Microsoft. During one such Think Week in October 1993, he surfed the internet for the first time. He also started hearing more and more reports from his staff about the Internet's growing popularity at universities.

Gradually, Bill began to recognize that the Internet was going to change the whole world of computing. In October 1994, he sent his executives a memo entitled "Sea change brings opportunity." ('Sea change' means a very big change.) In 1990, there had been one 'sea change' from the text-based user interface to the graphical user interface of Windows. "I believe we are in the midst of another major sea change," he wrote, "the move to electronic communication with office documents."

The Internet Tidal Wave

In May 1995, Bill sent out another executive memo called "The Internet Tidal Wave." From the name, it's clear that he was now taking the Internet very seriously indeed. The Internet was "an incredible opportunity as well as an incredible challenge" that would "change all the rules."

Right now, Microsoft was behind: Apple had QuickTime and Adobe had pdf, but none of Microsoft's applications had Internet-compatible formats. Everyone at Microsoft needed to start taking the Internet seriously before it was too late!

> *I assign the Internet the highest level of importance. In this memo, I want to make clear that our focus on the Internet is crucial to every part of our business. The Internet is the most important single*

development to come along since the IBM-PC was introduced in 1981. It is even more important than the arrival of the graphical user interface (GUI).

The browser wars begin

To get a presence on the Internet, Microsoft needed to build its own browser. In the summer of 1994, Microsoft began negotiating with Spyglass, the company which owned the official licensing rights for Mosaic, the browser which Marc Andreesen of Netscape had developed while at the University of Illinois. (There was a court battle between the university and Netscape about who owned the browser.)

In December 1994, Microsoft paid Spyglass $2 million to license the Mosaic browser. Licensing an existing browser was a faster way to catch up with Netscape than building a completely new browser. Eight months after the release of Netscape Navigator, Microsoft released Internet Explorer 1.0 in August 1995. Four months later, in December 1995, Bill held a press conference. In future, he said, everything Microsoft did would be built around the Internet. Internet Explorer would be given away for free and would work on both PCs and Macs.

By the middle of 1996, Microsoft's Internet division had grown to 2,500 employees. In August, Microsoft released Internet Explorer 3.0 free of charge bundled with the Windows 95 operating system. (Because Microsoft was not earning any revenue from the free browser, it stopped paying Spyglass the license fee. Spyglass had to take Microsoft to court to get the money it was owed!)

Microsoft now began using its market power to crush Netscape. It offered manufacturers discounts on Windows if they installed Internet Explorer on the computers they made. It also persuaded all the big online service providers—AOL, CompuServe et cetera—to choose Internet Explorer as the official browser for their millions of users.

As usual, Microsoft's merciless bullying tactics worked. In 1996, when Internet Explorer

3.0 was launched, its share was 3% versus 74% for Netscape. By September 1998, Microsoft had 48% of the market versus Netscape's 41%. By 1999, Netscape had been bought by AOL and was no longer an independent company!

Microsoft had won the First Browser War. All Netscape could do was complain to the government.

Fighting the government

The US government had already started worrying about Microsoft becoming too powerful in 1990. At the beginning, the government thought that Microsoft and IBM were planning to divide up the market for operating systems between them by making two parallel operating systems—MS-DOS for the lower end of the market and OS/2 for the high end. After IBM and Microsoft broke off their relationship in April 1991, this stopped being a problem.

The next thing the government objected to was the way Microsoft launched the Windows

3.0 OS at the same time as the applications Word, Excel and PowerPoint. As we saw earlier, this was mostly an accident, but it made Microsoft the leader both in operating systems and in applications. Was the company too powerful? Should it be broken up into two parts, an operating systems company and an applications company?

People felt that Bill Gates was in a similar position to John D. Rockefeller (1839–1937). Rockefeller was a millionaire businessman who had controlled *both* the oil wells that produced oil *and* the gas stations that sold it to motorists. Rockefeller, in other words, was a monopolist who had total control of his market, something that's usually not good for consumers. In 1911, the government forced Rockefeller to break up his company, Standard Oil, into 34 smaller companies.

Bill Gates was certainly just as rich as Rockefeller. In January 1993, the value of Microsoft passed that of IBM, and by July 1995 the 39-year-old Bill Gates was the richest man in the world.

Not Mr. Popular

Plenty of people had nasty things to say about Bill Gates. In the early 1990s, all sorts of companies were producing word-processing, spreadsheet and database applications for PCs. But as Microsoft became more and more successful, these companies got smaller and smaller.

Here is what some of Bill's competitors said about him.

"He's made business unprofitable for the rest of us. There is no balance of power. The notion of fairness means nothing to him."
—Philippe Kahn, CEO of Borland, a database company

"Microsoft is a threat to everyone in the industry."
—Alan Ashton, founder of WordPerfect Corporation, a word-processing company

"He is a user. He has taken much from me and the industry."

Part 3 World No. 1

—Gary Kildall, Digital Research, Inc., creator of the CP/M operating system

In 1998, the government accused Microsoft of engaging in anticompetitive practices so that it could keep its monopoly in PC operating systems and extend that monopoly to Internet browsing software. Here are some of the anticompetitive practices that the government accused Microsoft of:

- Offering Windows at a lower price to computer makers who also bought applications like Word and Excel.

- Forcing computer makers to include Internet Explorer along with Windows.

- Not separating the teams that developed the Windows OS and its applications. As a result, Microsoft developers knew how to make their applications work better with Windows than outside developers.

- Making computer makers pay them a "per processor" fee for every computer they sold, even if it did not contain DOS or Windows.

Gates fights back

Bill regarded the heads of the companies that complained about him as "bad losers." "We're being attacked because we're successful," he used to say. He argued that the legal actions of the government were a waste of taxpayer money and that everything Microsoft did was good for the consumer because it pushed down prices. Monopoly companies are supposed to put up prices. By giving away Internet Explorer for free, Microsoft had forced Netscape to start giving away its browser for free too. How was that bad?

An unlikely alliance

Since the government was investigating Microsoft for being an over-powerful monopoly, the last thing Bill wanted was for one of his biggest competitors to go out of business. By 1997, Apple was in a very bad state. Its market share in the United States was just 4.6% compared to 86% for Windows.

In January 1997, Apple rehired its co-founder Steve Jobs to rescue the company. At the Macworld conference in Boston in August, Jobs announced that he had accepted a $150 million investment from Microsoft. This investment was good news for Mac fans, but also good news for Bill, as it kept his only serious competitor in business.

Breaking up is hard to do

In November 1999, the judge in charge of the antitrust case declared that Microsoft was a monopoly. He called for the company to be split into an applications business and an operating systems business. The judge did not like Bill Gates as a person. He compared him to Napoleon and his staff to a drug gang!

Microsoft appealed. In 2002, the court decided that although Microsoft had abused its market power, it had not abused its customers, so there was no need to break up the company.

As often happens with government officials, their timing was exactly wrong. They were putting pressure on Microsoft just when it was about to start its decline and Apple was about to start its recovery.

Gates said that all the battles with the government and the damage to his reputation had made his job less enjoyable. Perhaps that is why he stepped down as CEO in 2000. Bill stayed on as chairman and chief software architect, while Steve Ballmer was appointed CEO.

Part 4

Bill Gates 2.0: The Philanthropist

Bill and Melinda receive the Presidential Medal of Freedom
© *ZUMA Press/amanaimages*

The birth of Saint Bill

Bill's career as a philanthropist started shortly after his mother's death in 1994, when he sold some Microsoft stock to create the William H. Gates Foundation. This foundation was named after his father, who also managed it.

With his wealth and power, people often compared Bill to the millionaires of late 19th century America. There was John D. Rockefeller, who controlled the oil business; Andrew Carnegie, who controlled the steel business; and J.P. Morgan who controlled the banking business. After becoming very rich—often not completely honestly—these three men started doing things for the public good in later life. Rockefeller focused on education and public health, Carnegie on libraries and universities, and Morgan on colleges and museums. Bill decided to follow their example and use his money to help others.

Bill was also coming under pressure. Not only did the government want to break up his company, political activists like Ralph Nader presented Bill as a symbol of social inequality. Gates's "net worth was equal to the net assets of the poorest 120 million Americans combined," Nader said. In such circumstances, for Bill to "repackage" himself as a nice philanthropist was a smart survival strategy.

The United States and beyond

In the beginning, the foundation was mostly active inside the United States. For example, the Gates Library Foundation provided money so that all public libraries in the U.S. could provide Internet access (on Microsoft computers, of course!). The Gates Millennium Scholars Program provides around 1,000 minority students with funding for university studies. The Sound Families Initiative tried to reduce the number of homeless families in Washington State, the Gates family's home state.

However, Bill and Melinda's philanthropic

activities were not limited to the United States for long. In 1997, they read a newspaper article that made a strong impression on them. It explained that easy-to-cure diseases like diarrhea, pneumonia, and malaria killed millions of people every year in the developing world. In rich countries, pharmaceutical companies spent millions of dollars to make drugs to treat unimportant problems like hair loss and impotence. Meanwhile, children in Africa were dying just because they were poor.

Bill and Melinda cut the article out of the paper and sent it to Bill's dad with a note: "Dad, maybe we can do something about this."

Bill and Melinda clearly saw that the problems in the United States and the problems in the developing world were different. In the United States, some children don't get the education they need to succeed. In the developing world, children are killed by diseases which have been eliminated in rich countries. They decided that their priorities would be education at home and health abroad.

The Bill & Melinda Gates Foundation

In 2000, the year that Bill gave up his CEO job, he merged the William H. Gates Foundation and the Gates Learning Foundation to form a new foundation: The Bill & Melinda Gates Foundation. With Steve Ballmer running Microsoft, Bill could give more time to his philanthropic work.

The approach Bill took was systematic and business-like. His strategy was to identify the diseases that cause the most deaths and concentrate on eliminating them. When Bill and Melinda started the foundation, Bill's friend Warren Buffett gave them some advice. "Don't just go for safe projects," he said. "Take on the really tough problems."

The goals of the foundation are certainly big and brave. They include the complete elimination of malaria, polio, tuberculosis and HIV; the reduction of malnutrition; and the promotion of birth control.

The Bill & Melinda Gates Foundation is now the largest philanthropic organization in the world. Its budget is larger than the World Health Organization. The foundation is funded not just by Bill's own fortune, but by money from his friend Warren Buffett, the investor. When Buffett donated $30 billion in 2006, he doubled the spending power of the foundation.

"Persons of the Year"

Bill's philanthropic work did help to change his image. In the 1990s, he was seen as a pitiless businessman, crushing all his competitors. In the 2000s, he became a smart fighter for the world's poor, crushing deadly diseases!

In December 2005, Bill and Melinda, together with Bono, the singer of U2, were chosen as "Persons of the Year" by *Time* magazine for their charitable work. Instead of going to the COMDEX computer show in Las Vegas every year, Bill started going to the World Economic Forum (WEF) at Davos in Switzerland. There Bill can talk about health and development issues to the world's most influential politicians, business leaders, academics and journalists.

Full-time philanthropist

In July 2008, Bill resigned as chief software architect at Microsoft (although he stayed on as chairman). After 33 years, he was no longer involved with running the company day-to-day. Wasn't he going to get bored?

"If I didn't have the foundation, which is so exciting and complex, leaving Microsoft would be tough for me," Bill joked. "I am not a sit-on-the-beach type of person."

At Davos that year, Bill gave a speech. "I am an impatient optimist. The world is getting better, but it's not getting better fast enough and it's not getting better for everyone," he said. He encouraged business leaders to use market-driven approaches to lift communities out of poverty.

The phrase "impatient optimist" is now the tagline of the foundation: "We are impatient optimists working to reduce inequity."

"Impatient optimists" is also the name of the blog of the Bill & Melinda Gates Foundation (impatientoptimists.org).

Bill & Melinda Gates Foundation Online

As you would expect with a foundation set up by a software pioneer, the Bill & Melinda Gates Foundation has an excellent website. Just as companies produce an annual shareholders report, Bill and Melinda produce an annual letter about their foundation. Full of graphics and photos, it gives a very clear idea about the foundation's goals and achievements. Reflecting Bill's interest in metrics, there are lots of numbers, percentages and graphs.

The 2017 Annual Letter, for example, says that global vaccine coverage is at 86%, its highest ever. It points out that one dollar spent on immunization in childhood delivers $44 in economic benefits later. Sometimes the statistics are quite exciting. For instance, in 1988 there were 350,000 new cases of polio. In 2016, partly thanks to Bill and Melinda, that number was down to *just 37 cases in three countries*!

Bill and Melinda believe that achieving dramatic results—getting a disease to zero—gets people excited and inspires them to try to eliminate more diseases.

You get a sense of how ambitious Bill and Melinda are from last paragraph of the 2017 annual letter. "Polio will soon be history," it says. "In our lifetimes, malaria will end. No one will die from AIDS. Few people will get TB. Children everywhere will be well nourished. And the death of a child in the developing world will be just as rare as the death of a child in the rich world."

On the whole, everyone admires the Gates Foundation's work on health and development. Some left-wing critics, however, think it is not right for a private organization to have so much influence on education in the United States.

Microsoft in decline

Not everyone at Microsoft was happy when Bill appointed Steve Ballmer CEO in 2000. Ballmer had spent 20 years working as Bill's right-hand man (or yes-man) and was not a software engineer. Was he the right person to lead the company?

Microsoft was becoming a bigger and bigger operation: in 1990, when Windows 3.0 came out, it had under 6,000 employees; by 2000, that number was closer to 40,000.

Windows 3.0 was the result of two engineers secretly creating a better operating system without telling their bosses. It was only approved *after* it was finished. As Microsoft got bigger, the crazy little startup started to become more bureaucratic, rigid—more like IBM, in short. It became the sort of place where people followed the rules and lucky accidents like Windows 3.0 could no longer happen.

In 1990, Microsoft introduced a performance review system called stacked ranking.

Under this system, some people on every team had to be graded as "below average" and "poor," even if they were all very good. Poor workers could be fired.

What effect did this system have? The best programmers in Microsoft stopped wanting to work together. It was much better for your career to work with people who were worse at their job than you. This meant that the output of the company got worse and worse. This was happening just when Apple was getting stronger and stronger and new companies like Google—founded in 1998—were challenging Microsoft in other areas.

A comedy of errors

Here are some of the mistakes Microsoft made. Most of them are from between 2000 and 2014, the years when Steve Ballmer was CEO.

- Microsoft developed an e-reader in 1998, six years before Sony and nine before Amazon. Bill shut down the project because the interface "did not look like Windows."

- Apple launched the iPod music player in 2001. Microsoft responded five years later with the Zune music player. It was discontinued in 2011 due to lack of demand.

- Microsoft became slow at developing software. There was a five-year gap between Windows XP (August 2001) and Windows Vista (November 2006)

- When Apple launched the iPhone in 2008, Steve Ballmer said "There's no chance it will get any significant market share." In fact, it was Windows Phone that never got any serious market share!

- Microsoft started losing market share in browsers. Internet Explorer's 80% share in 2002 fell as low as 15% in 2012 because of competition from new browsers like Firefox and Chrome.

- Microsoft's favorite technique of copying other company's software and then forcefully taking control of the market stopped working. Bing, the search engine Microsoft unveiled in 2009, never came close to Google.

- Microsoft started buying other companies in expensive deals that often failed. In 2013, for example, it paid $7.9 billion for the phone unit of the phone maker Nokia. One year later it took an impairment charge of $7.6 billion. In other words, Nokia was almost worthless.

Microsoft did have a few successes under Steve Ballmer. For example, both the Xbox gaming console (2001) and the Azure cloud-computing brand (2010) have grown into large businesses.

Best man: Worst CEO

The failure of the Nokia acquisition was a step too far. In 2014, Bill, who was still chairman, asked Steve Ballmer to step down as CEO. The 57-year-old Ballmer was replaced by Satya Nadella, an Indian who had been at Microsoft since 1992. Eleven years younger than Ballmer, Nadella was in charge of the Cloud and Enterprise Group. Bill described him as "a proven leader with hardcore engineering skills, business vision and the ability to bring people together." (Bill stepped down as chairman at the same time.)

The Nadella effect

For a long time, the culture at Microsoft reflected Bill Gates's character. It was intense, competitive and bullying. That was okay when the company was fighting its way to the top, or enjoyed complete control of the PC desktop. It was not an attitude that worked in the fluid and collaborative multiplatform world of mobile apps.

The first thing Satya Nadella did was to change this culture. He wanted to collaborate with other companies not to crush them. Under Nadella's leadership, Microsoft stopped trying to make Windows the center of everything. It joined the open source Linux Foundation, released Microsoft Office for iPad, released apps for Android and iOS and introduced cool hardware like the Microsoft Surface Book laptop.

As soon as Nadella was made CEO, the stock price of Microsoft started to shoot up, eventually doubling by mid-2017. Funnily enough, it was Steve Ballmer who benefited the most, because he owns more stock in the company than even Bill!

The Gates family

Bill and Melinda have three children; Jennifer, born in 1996, Rory, born in 1999, and Phoebe, born in 2002. They do their best to keep their private life private. For example, when they talk about their children in public, they try to refer to them as "our son" or "our youngest daughter," rather than using their names. They are trying to give them a normal upbringing.

"They are normal kids," says Bill. "They help with the household chores. They get pocket money." Bill is not planning to leave them a lot of money. As adults, he wants them to work like everybody else.

Bill and Melinda seem to enjoy working together. They are both very smart, able to absorb information fast, and are good critical thinkers. "She and I enjoy sharing ideas and talking about what we are learning," says Bill. "When one of us is being very optimistic, the other takes on the role of making sure we're thinking through all the tough issues."

Billionaires of the world, unite!

In 2010, Bill and Melinda teamed up with Gates's old friend Warren Buffett to found the Giving Pledge. The Giving Pledge is a campaign that encourages the world's richest people to give away half their wealth to philanthropic causes. Because many people admire Buffett and Bill and Melinda, the campaign has been very successful. As of 2017, 170 people from 21 countries had promised to give away their money. They included Mark Zuckerberg of Facebook, Reed Hastings of Netflix, and George Lucas, the creator of *Star Wars*.

Investing and thinking

These days, Bill only owns about 4% of Microsoft. Most of his money is in his private investment company Cascade Investment. Among other things, Cascade owns nearly 50% of the Four Seasons Hotel group; almost 10% of tractor maker Deere; and over 4,000 shares in Warren Buffett's company, Berkshire Hathaway (Since one share costs around $270,000, that's quite a lot of money!)

Bill is now a public intellectual who writes essays to influence government policy and public opinion. If you want to know what he is thinking, you can go to LinkedIn (where he has been posting articles since 2013) or to his personal blog, Gates Notes. His favorite subjects to write about are education, new energy, philanthropy and books that he has enjoyed.

Honored by the president

In November 2016, Barack Obama invited Bill and Melinda to the White House to receive the Presidential Medal of Freedom, the highest non-military honor. Perhaps as a mark of respect, they were the first people to receive their medal, ahead of 19 other people including Robert Redford, Robert De Niro and Bruce Springsteen.

"For two decades, the Gates Foundation has worked to provide lifesaving medical care to millions," said President Obama. "Bill and Melinda have donated more money to charitable causes than anyone ever. Many years ago, Melinda's mom told her an old saying: 'To know that even one person's life has been easier because of you is a success.' By this and just about any other measure, few in human history have been more successful than these two impatient optimists."

Bill Gates has been exceptionally successful in both acts of his remarkable life, first as a businessperson and then as a philanthropist.

THE END

Word List

- LEVEL 1, 2は本文で使われている全ての語を掲載しています。
  LEVEL 3以上は、中学校レベルの語を含みません。ただし、本文で特殊な意味で使われている場合、その意味のみを掲載しています。
- 語形が規則変化する語の見出しは原形で示しています。不規則変化語は本文中で使われている形になっています。
- 一般的な意味を紹介していますので、一部の語で本文で実際に使われている品詞や意味と合っていないことがあります。
- 品詞は以下のように示しています。

名 名詞	代 代名詞	形 形容詞	副 副詞	動 動詞	助 助動詞
前 前置詞	接 接続詞	間 間投詞	冠 冠詞	略 略語	俗 俗語
熟 熟語	頭 接頭語	尾 接尾語	号 記号	関 関係代名詞	

A

- □ **ability** 名 才能
- □ **about to** 《be-》まさに~しようとしている、~するところだ
- □ **absence** 名 欠席 take a leave of absence 休学する
- □ **absorb** 動 吸収する
- □ **abuse** 動 悪用する
- □ **academic** 名 学者
- □ **accept** 動 受け入れる
- □ **access** 名 (システムなどへの)アクセス、アクセス権 動 アクセスする
- □ **accident** 名 偶然
- □ **accidental** 形 偶然の
- □ **according to** ①~によれば[よると] ②~に従って
- □ **accuse A of** ~の理由でAを非難する
- □ **accustomed to** 《be-》~が習慣になっている
- □ **achieve** 動 成功を収める
- □ **achievement** 名 達成
- □ **acquisition** 名 獲得
- □ **acre** 名 エーカー《面積の単位、約4,046.7平方メートル》
- □ **act** 名 行為 動 ①行動する ②演技をする
- □ **active** 形 活動中の
- □ **activist** 名 活動家
- □ **activity** 名 活動
- □ **actually** 副 実際に、本当に、実は
- □ **ad** 略 advertisement (広告、宣伝)の略 classified ad (新聞などの)案内広告
- □ **add** 動 加える、足す
- □ **addition** 熟 in addition 加えて、さらに
- □ **administrator** 名 管理者、理事
- □ **admire** 動 賞賛する
- □ **Adobe** 名 アドビ・システムズ《社名》
- □ **adult** 名 大人
- □ **advance** 名 前払い金 動 ①促進する ②昇進する
- □ **advantage** 名 有利な立場
- □ **advertising** 名 広告、宣伝
- □ **advice** 名 助言
- □ **Aerosmith** 名 エアロスミス《アメリカのロックバンド》
- □ **affordable** 形 手ごろな価格の
- □ **Africa** 名 アフリカ《大陸》
- □ **after that** その後

Word List

- **afterward** 副 のちに
- **age** 熟 at the age of ～歳のときに
- **agency** 名 機関
- **agree with** (人)に同意する
- **agreement** 名 合意
- **ahead of** ～に先んじて
- **AIDS** 略 エイズ, 後天性免疫不全症候群 (= acquired immune acquired immune)
- **aim** 動 ねらう, 目指す
- **air-conditioning** 名 空調設備
- **airplane** 名 飛行機
- **Alan Ashton** アラン・アシュトン《人名》
- **Albuquerque** 名 アルバカーキ《米国の地名》
- **ale** 名 ginger ale ジンジャーエール
- **all the time** いつも, その間ずっと
- **(That is about) all.** (話すことは)それくらいです。
- **all-day** 形 終日の
- **alliance** 名 同盟, 提携
- **allow A to** Aが～するのを可能にする, Aに～させておく
- **along with** ～と一緒に
- **Altair** 名 アルテア《MITS社が開発した世界最初の家庭用コンピューター》
- **although** 接 ～だけれども, ～にもかかわらず, たとえ～でも
- **always** 熟 not always 必ずしも～であるとは限らない
- **amazed** 形 驚いた
- **amazing** 形 驚くべき, 見事な
- **Amazon Prime** アマゾン・プライム《Amazonの有料会員制プログラム》
- **Amazon.com** 名 アマゾン・ドット・コム《社名》
- **ambitious** 形 大望のある
- **America** 名 アメリカ《国名・大陸》
- **American** 名 アメリカ人
- **amid** 前 ～の最中に
- **analyze** 動 分析する, 解析する
- **and so on** ～など, その他もろもろ
- **Andrew Carnegie** アンドリュー・カーネギー《アメリカの実業家, 1835–1919》
- **Android** 名 アンドロイド《携帯情報端末向けOS》
- **Annie Leibovitz** アニー・リーボヴィッツ《人名》
- **announce** 動 公表する
- **annual** 形 年1回の, 例年の 名 年報
- **another** 熟 one another お互い
- **anticompetitive** 形 反競争的な
- **antitrust** 形 独占禁止の
- **anymore** 副《通例否定文, 疑問文で》今はもう, これ以上
- **anyone** 代 ①《疑問文・条件節で》誰か ②《否定文で》誰も (～ない) ③《肯定文で》誰でも
- **anyway** 副 どうしても
- **anywhere** 副 どこでも
- **AOL** 名 エーオーエル《社名》
- **apartment** 名 アパート
- **app** 略 アプリ (= application program)
- **appeal** 動 (人を)惹き付ける 名 魅力
- **application** 名 アプリケーション
- **apply** 動 出願する
- **appoint** 動 任命する
- **approach** 名 やり方, アプローチ
- **approve** 動 承認する
- **architect** 名 設計者
- **architecture** 名 構成, 構造 open-architecture オープン・アーキテクチャ《ハードやソフトの仕様を一般公開して, 誰もがそれに準じた製品を

The Bill Gates Story

作れるようにすること》
- **argue** 動 ①議論する ②主張する
- **argument** 名 ①論争 ②論拠
- **arrange** 動 手はずを整える
- **arrival** 名 到着
- **art of** ～術
- **article** 名 (新聞・雑誌などの)記事
- **as** 熟 as if あたかも～のように, まるで～みたいに just as ～と同程度に
- **assemble** 動 組み立てる
- **asset** 名 資産 net asset 純資産
- **assign** 動 ～を割り当てる
- **astonish** 動 びっくりさせる
- **attack** 動 攻撃する
- **attention** 名 注意
- **attitude** 名 姿勢, 態度
- **Auckland** 名 オークランド《ニュージーランドの地名》
- **audio** 形 音声の, オーディオの
- **authority** 名《the -ties》(関係)当局
- **automobile** 名 自動車
- **available** 形 利用[使用・入手]できる
- **average** 名 平均(値)
- **avoid** 動 避ける, (～を)しないようにする
- **award** 動 授与する
- **Azure** 名 アジュール《マイクロソフトのクラウド構築システム》

B

- **bachelor** 名 独身男性
- **back** 熟 get back 戻る, 帰る go back to ～に帰る[戻る] rock back and forth 前後に揺らす
- **balance** 名 均衡
- **banker** 名 銀行家[員]
- **banking** 名 銀行業
- **Barack Obama** バラク・オバマ《アメリカ第44代大統領》
- **base** 動 ～に本拠地を置く
- **BASIC** 略 ベーシック (= beginner's all-purpose symbolic instruction code)《プログラミング言語》
- **battle** 名 戦い
- **bay** 名 湾
- **beard** 名 あごひげ
- **because of** ～のために, ～の理由で
- **bedroom** 名 寝室
- **begin with** ～で始まる
- **beginning** 名 初め, 始まり
- **behave** 動 振る舞う
- **behavior** 名 態度
- **behind** 前 ～に遅れて, ～に劣って 副 後ろに, 遅れて be left behind 後れを取る get behind 後れを取る
- **belief** 名 信念
- **believe in** ～を信じる
- **belong to** ～に属する
- **below** 前 ～以下の, ～より劣る
- **benefit** 名 利益 動 利益を得る, (～の)ためになる
- **Berkshire Hathaway** バークシャー・ハサウェイ《社名》
- **beside** 前 ～と並んで
- **best** 熟 do one's best 全力を尽くす
- **bestseller** 名 ベストセラー
- **bet** 動 賭ける
- **better** 熟 get better (病気などが)良くなる
- **between A and B** AとBの間に
- **beyond** 前 ～を越えて, ～の向こうに
- **Bible** 名《the -》聖書
- **Big Blue** ビッグ・ブルー《IBM社の愛称》

Word List

- **Bill & Melinda Gates Foundation** ビル＆メリンダ・ゲイツ財団
- **Bill Gates** ビル・ゲイツ《人名》
- **billion** 名 10億
- **billionaire** 名 億万長者
- **Bing** 名 ビング《マイクロソフトの検索エンジン》
- **birth** 名 ①誕生 ②出産
- **bit** 名《a–》少し
- **blanket** 名 毛布
- **blew** 動 blow(吹き飛ばす)の過去
- **blink** 動 点滅する
- **blog** 名 ブログ
- **blood** 名 血統
- **blow** 動 ～を吹き飛ばす
- **board** 名 ①板 ②委員会, 重役会 board game ボードゲーム
- **Bono** 名 ボノ《ロックバンド, U2のリードボーカル》
- **boot** 動 起動する
- **bored** 形 うんざりした, 退屈した
- **boring** 形 うんざりさせる, 退屈な
- **Borland** 名 ボーランド《社名》
- **Borsheim's** 名 ボーシャイム《社名》
- **boss** 名 上司
- **Boston** 名 ボストン《米国の地名》
- **both A and B** AもBも
- **boyhood** 名 少年時代
- **boys-only** 形 男子だけの
- **Brad Pitt** ブラッド・ピット《アメリカの俳優》
- **brand** 名 ブランド, 商標
- **brave** 形 勇敢な
- **break into** ～に押し入る
- **break up** 分割する, ばらばらにする
- **breast** 名 乳房
- **brick** 形 レンガ造りの
- **brilliant** 形 光り輝く, すばらしい
- **broadband** 形 広帯域の, ブロードバンドの
- **browse** 動 (インターネット上の情報を)閲覧する
- **browser** 名 (インターネットの)ブラウザ, 閲覧ソフト
- **Bruce Springsteen** ブルース・スプリングスティーン《アメリカのシンガーソングライター》
- **budget** 名 予算
- **bug** 名 (ソフト・プログラムの)不具合, バグ
- **building** 名 建物
- **bully** 動 いじめる
- **bundle** 動 (複数の商品を)セット売りする
- **bunker** 名 貯蔵庫, 掩蔽壕(えんぺいごう)
- **bureaucratic** 形 お役所的な
- **business-like** 形 実務的な
- **businessman** 名 ビジネスマン, 実業家

C

- **cable** 名 ケーブル
- **calculator** 名 計算機
- **California** 名 カリフォルニア《米国の州》
- **Californian** 形 カリフォルニアの
- **call for** ～を求める
- **calmly** 副 落ち着いて
- **Cambridge** 名 ケンブリッジ大学
- **camera** 名 カメラ
- **campaign** 名 キャンペーン(活動, 運動)
- **campus** 名 キャンパス, (大学などの)構内
- **cancer** 名 がん
- **cannibalize** 動 共食いをする, 自

社製品の売り上げを食う
- **capability** 图機能, 性能
- **capture** 動(競争で)〜を勝ち取る
- **care about** 〜を気に掛ける
- **career** 图経歴, キャリア
- **Caribbean** 图カリブ海
- **carpark** 图駐車場
- **Cascade Investment** カスケード・インベストメント《社名》
- **Castle and Cooke Properties** キャッスル&クック不動産《社名》
- **catch up with** 〜に追いつく
- **category** 图種類, カテゴリー
- **cause** 〜を引き起こす, 〜の原因となる 图目的
- **CD-Rom** 略シーディーロム(= compact disc read only memory)
- **ceiling** 图天井
- **celebrate** 動祝杯を挙げる
- **cent** 图セント《米国などの通貨単位。1ドルの100分の1》
- **CEO** 略最高経営責任者(= Chief Executive Officer)
- **ceremony** 图式典
- **certainly** 副確かに, 必ず
- **chairman** 图会長
- **challenge** 图挑戦 動挑む
- **change** 图 sea change 大転換, 様変わり
- **chapel** 图礼拝堂
- **chapter** 图(書物の)章
- **character** 图個性
- **charge** 图(代金を)請求する 图①請求金額, 料金 ②責任 **in charge of** 〜を任されて, 〜を担当して
- **charitable** 形慈善のための
- **charity** 图慈善(行為)
- **Charles Foster Kane** チャールズ・フォスター・ケーン《架空のキャラクター, 新聞王》
- **Charles Simonyi** チャールズ・シモニー《人名》
- **cheaply** 副安く
- **chemistry** 图化学
- **cherry** 图サクランボ
- **chief** 图主任
- **childhood** 图幼児期
- **chip** 图半導体小片
- **choice** 图選択
- **chore** 图雑用
- **chosen as** 《be-》〜として選ばれる
- **Chris Larson** クリス・ラーソン《人名》
- **Chrome** 图クローム《グーグルのウェブブラウザ》
- **circumstance** 图《-s》(人の)境遇
- **Citizen Kane** 『市民ケーン』《アメリカの映画, 1941》
- **classified ad** (新聞などの)案内広告
- **clear** 形はっきりした, 明白な
- **clearly** 副はっきりと, 明らかに
- **clever** 形頭のよい
- **clip** 動(クリップなどで)留める
- **Clockwork Orange** 《A-》『時計じかけのオレンジ』《イギリスの映画, 1971》
- **clone** 图同型のもの, 複製品
- **clone-killer** 形同型殺しの, 同型品を駆逐する
- **closer to** 〜にさらに近づいて
- **cloud-computing** 图クラウドコンピューティング《ネットを最大限に活用するコンピューター利用形態》
- **COBOL** 略コボル(= Common Business Oriented Language)《プログラミング言語》
- **code** 图コード, プログラム 動プ

Word List

ログラムする source code ソース・コード

- □ **coding** 名 コーディング, プログラミング
- □ **Codex Leicester** レスター手稿《レオナルド・ダ・ヴィンチ手書きのノート》
- □ **co-founder** 名 共同創立者
- □ **collaborate** 動 共同する, 合作する
- □ **collaborative** 形 協力的な
- □ **colleague** 名 同僚
- □ **Columbia River** コロンビア川
- □ **combination** 名 組み合わせ
- □ **combine** 動 結合する
- □ **COMDEX** 名 コムデックス《コンピューターの展示会》
- □ **come** 熟 come along 現れる come back 戻る come back to ~に戻る come out 世に出る, 発表される, 発行される come out of ~から出てくる
- □ **comedian** 名 喜劇役者, コメディアン
- □ **comedy** 名 ①コメディー ②喜劇的場面
- □ **comfortable** 形 快適な, 心地いい
- □ **coming** 形 今度の
- □ **command** 名 指示, コマンド
- □ **comment** 動 論評する, コメントする
- □ **Commodore** 名 コモドール《社名》
- □ **communication** 名 やり取り, コミュニケーション
- □ **communist** 名 共産主義者
- □ **community** 名 ①地域社会 ②《the ~》社会(一般), 世間
- □ **Compaq** 名 コンパック《社名》
- □ **compare** 動 ①比較する ②たとえる be compared to ~と比較して, ~に比べれば
- □ **compatible** 形 ~準拠の, 互換性のある
- □ **competing** 形 競合する
- □ **competition** 名 ①コンテスト ②競合
- □ **competitive** 形 競争心の強い
- □ **competitor** 名 競争相手
- □ **complain** 動 不平[苦情]を言う
- □ **complete** 形 完全な, まったくの 動 完成させる
- □ **completely** 副 完全に, すっかり
- □ **complex** 形 複雑な
- □ **complicated** 形 複雑な
- □ **CompuServe** 名 コンピュサーブ《社名, 同社が提供する通信サービス名》
- □ **Computer Center Corporation** コンピューター・センター・コーポレーション《社名》
- □ **computing** 形 コンピューターの, コンピューター関係の
- □ **concentrate** 動 集中する, 専心する
- □ **concern** 動 気にする
- □ **conference** 名 会議, 協議 press conference 記者会見
- □ **connection** 名 つながり, 関係
- □ **conquer** 動 制圧する
- □ **conservatively** 副 保守的に, 控えめに
- □ **console** 名 制御盤, コンソール
- □ **consumer** 名 消費者 consumer goods 消費財
- □ **contain** 動 含む, 入っている
- □ **content** 名 内容, コンテンツ
- □ **contract** 名 契約(書)
- □ **contribution** 名 保険料 social security contributions 社会保険負担
- □ **control** 動 管理[支配]する 名 管理, 支配(力) in control 主導権を握って take control of ~を制御[支配]する
- □ **conversation** 名 会話

THE BILL GATES STORY

- **convince** 動 納得させる
- **copy** 名 ①写し, コピー ②(本やソフトなどの)一部, 冊 動 複写する, コピーする, まねる
- **corporation** 名 法人, (株式)会社
- **correctly** 副 正確に
- **cost** 動 (金・費用が)かかる, (〜を)要する
- **count** 動 数える
- **countryside** 名 地方, 田舎
- **couple of** 《a-》2, 3の
- **course** 熟 of course もちろん, 当然
- **court** 名 ①(球技の)コート ②法廷, 裁判所
- **cover** 動 覆う 名 (本などの)表紙
- **coverage** 名 被覆率
- **co-writer** 名 共著者
- **CP/M** 略 シーピーエム (= Control Program/Microprocessors)《デジタル・リサーチ社のOS》
- **CP/M-86** 略 シーピーエム86《デジタル・リサーチ社のOS》
- **crash** 名 (コンピューターの)機能停止, クラッシュ
- **crazy** 形 奇妙な, 常軌を逸した 名 狂人
- **create** 動 創造する, 生み出す, 引き起こす
- **creator** 名 創作者
- **critic** 名 批評家, 評論家
- **critical** 形 批判的な
- **crucial** 形 重大な, 決定的な
- **crush** 動 〜を壊滅させる, 押しつぶす
- **Cupertino** 名 クパチーノ《アメリカの地名》
- **customer** 名 顧客
- **cut ~ out** 〜を切り抜く

D

- **Dallas** 名 ダラス《アメリカの地名》
- **damage** 名 損害
- **dangerously** 副 危険なほどに
- **DARPA** 略 ダーパ, アメリカ国防総省国防高等研究事業局 (= Defense Advanced Research Projects Agency)
- **data** 名 情報, データ
- **Data General Corp.** データゼネラル《社名》
- **database** 名 データベース
- **Davos** 名 ダボス《スイスの地名》
- **dawn** 名 夜明け
- **day** 熟 day and night 昼も夜も in those days あのころは, 当時は one day (過去の)ある日, (未来の)いつか these days このごろ
- **day-to-day** 副 毎日, 日常的に
- **deadly** 形 命にかかわる
- **deal** 名 取引, 契約
- **death** 名 死
- **debt** 名 負債 be in debt 借金している
- **debug** 動 〜の欠陥を探して直す, デバッグする
- **debut** 動 初登場する, デビューする
- **DEC** 略 デジタル・イクイップメント社 (= Digital Equipment Corporation)
- **decade** 名 10年間
- **decide to do** 〜することに決める
- **decision** 名 決定
- **declare** 動 宣言する
- **decline** 名 下り坂, 衰え
- **deeply** 副 深く
- **Deere** 名 ディア《社名》
- **Defense Advanced Research Projects Agency**

Word List

アメリカ国防総省国防高等研究事業局
- **degree** 名(大学の)学位 undergraduate degree 学士号
- **deliver** 動 ①配達する ②達成する,果たす
- **Dell** 名デル《社名》
- **demand** 動要求する 名需要
- **demanding** 形要求が厳しい
- **demonstrate** 動実演する
- **demonstration** 名実演,デモンストレーション
- **dependent on** ～に左右される,～に依存している
- **describe** 動(言葉で)描写する,説明する
- **desert** 名砂漠
- **design** 動企てる 名デザイン,設計
- **desktop** 名デスクトップ,コンピューターの初期画面 形デスクトップの
- **destiny** 名運命
- **destroy** 動破壊する
- **develop** 動①開発する ②発展する
- **developer** 名開発者
- **developing world** 発展途上世界
- **development** 名①発展 ②開発
- **diarrhea** 名下痢
- **die** 動死ぬ
- **digital** 形デジタルの
- **Digital Equipment Corporation** デジタル・イクイップメント社《社名》
- **Digital Research, Inc.** デジタル・リサーチ社《社名》
- **direct** 形直接の
- **direction** 名方向,目標
- **directly** 副直接に
- **director** 名監督
- **disagree** 動反対する
- **disappear** 動姿を消す
- **discontinue** 動製造を中止する
- **discount** 名割引
- **discussion** 名討論
- **disease** 名病気
- **dislocation** 名混乱
- **display** 動展示する,示す
- **disruption** 名(外的要因による)崩壊
- **divide up** 分割する
- **division** 名部門
- **do one's best** 全力を尽くす
- **do with** ～を処理する
- **doctorate** 名博士号 honorary doctorate 名誉博士号
- **document** 名文書,ドキュメント・ファイル
- **dominant** 形支配的な
- **donate** 動寄付する
- **dorm** 名寮,寄宿舎
- **DOS** 略ディスク・オペレーティング・システム(= disk operating system)
- **double** 動2倍になる[する]
- **download** 動ダウンロードする
- **dramatic** 形劇的な
- **draw** 動(結論などを)出す,引用する
- **dream of** ～を夢見る
- **drive** 動車で行く
- **drop out** 中退する
- **drop out of** ～から中退する
- **drove** 動drive (車で行く)の過去
- **drug** 名医薬,麻薬 drug gang 麻薬密売人
- **due to** ～によって,～が原因で
- **Duke University** デューク大学
- **dying** 動die (死ぬ)の現在分詞

E

- **earn** 動 儲ける, 稼ぐ
- **easily** 副 容易に, 気楽に
- **easy-to-cure** 形 簡単に治せる
- **e-commerce** 名 電子[インターネット]商取引
- **economic** 形 経済学の, 経済上の
- **Ed Roberts** エド・ロバーツ《人名》
- **edition** 名 (本・雑誌などの)版
- **education** 名 教育, 教養
- **effect** 名 影響, 効果
- **effort** 名 努力(の成果)
- **either A or B** AかそれともB
- **electric** 形 電気の, 電動の
  electric power comany 電力会社
- **electrical** 形 電気の, 電気製品の
  electrical grid 配電網
- **electronic** 形 電子工学の, エレクトロニクスの
- **electronics** 名 電子工学, 電子機器
- **eliminate** 動 撲滅する
- **elimination** 名 排除
- **Elizabeth Gates** 名 エリザベス・ゲイツ《人名》
- **e-mail** 名 電子メール
- **embark** 動 着手する
- **Empire State Building** エンパイア・ステート・ビルディング《高層ビル》
- **employ** 動 (人を)雇う
- **employee** 名 従業員
- **emulate** 動 (他のプログラムを)エミュレートする
- **emulation** 名 エミュレーション《プログラムなどを, 本来とは異なる環境のコンピューターで, 擬似的に同じ環境を作って使うこと》
- **enable** 動 (～することを)可能にする
- **Encarta** 名 エンカルタ《マイクロソフトが製作し, 販売していた電子百科事典》
- **encounter** 動 (思いがけなく)出会う 名 遭遇
- **encourage** 動 勧める, 働きかける
- **encyclopedia** 名 百科事典
- **end** 熟 end up (最後には) ～になる in the end とうとう, 結局, ついに
- **engage** 動《be -d in》～に従事している
- **engagement** 名 婚約
- **engine** 名 (精巧な)機械装置
  search engine 検索ソフト
- **engineer** 名 技師
- **engineering** 名 工学
- **enjoy doing** ～するのが好きだ, ～するのを楽しむ
- **enjoyable** 形 楽しめる, 愉快な
- **enlarged** 形 拡大された
- **enormously** 副 巨大に
- **enough to do** ～するのに十分な
- **enroll** 動 入学する
- **enterprise** 名 企業
- **entertainment** 名 娯楽, 歓待
- **entire** 形 全体の
- **entitle** 動 ～に題名をつける
- **entrepreneur** 名 企業家, 起業家
- **environment** 名 環境
- **equal to**《be -》～に等しい
- **equipment** 名 装置, 設備
- **e-reader** 名 電子書籍
- **Eric Bina** エリック・ビーナ《人名》
- **error** 名 失策, 誤り
- **essay** 名 随筆, エッセイ
- **estate** 名 不動産
- **et cetera** 副 その他, ～など
- **even if** たとえ～でも
- **even though** ～であるけれども,

WORD LIST

～にもかかわらず
- **eventually** 副 結局は
- **ever since** それ以来ずっと
- **every time** ～するときはいつも
- **everybody** 代 誰でも, 皆
- **everyone** 代 誰でも, 皆
- **everything** 代 すべてのこと[もの], 何もかも
- **everywhere** 副 どこでも
- **exam** 名《略式》試験
- **example** 熟 for example たとえば
- **Excel** 名 エクセル《マイクロソフトの表計算ソフト》
- **excellent** 形 優れた
- **except for** ～を除いて
- **exceptionally** 副 非常に
- **excited** 形 興奮した, わくわくした
- **exciting** 形 興奮させる, わくわくさせる
- **exclude** 動 排除する
- **executive** 名 重役, 役員
- **exhibition** 名 展示会, 見本市
- **existing** 形 従来の, 既存の
- **expand** 動 拡張[発展]する
- **expect** 動 予期[予測]する, (当然のこととして)期待する
- **Expedia** 名 エクスペディア《旅行予約サイト》
- **expel** 動 除名する
- **experiment** 名 実験 動 試みる
- **explorer** 名 探検者 Internet Explorer インターネット・エクスプローラー《マイクロソフトのウェブブラウザ》
- **expression** 名 言い回し, 表現
- **extend** 動 (範囲が)およぶ, 広がる
- **exterior** 名 外側
- **extremely** 副 極度に

F

- **Facebook** 名 フェイスブック《SNS》
- **fact** 熟 in fact 実際には, 実際, 要するに, それどころか
- **fade** 動 衰える
- **fail** 動 ①失敗する ②《– to》～し損なう, ～できない
- **failure** 名 失敗
- **fair** 形 公平[正当]な
- **fairness** 名 公平さ
- **fantastic** 形 奇想天外な, すばらしい
- **far** 熟 as far as ～する限りでは
- **fatal** 形 致命的な
- **fault** 名 過失, 誤り
- **fax** 名 ファックス
- **feature** 名 外観
- **featuring** 形 主演の
- **fee** 名 料金
- **female** 形 女性の
- **Ferris wheel** 大観覧車
- **few** 熟 quite a few かなり多くの
- **fierce** 形 すさまじい
- **fight back** 反撃に転じる, 応戦する
- **fighter** 名 戦士
- **figure ~ out** ～を理解する
- **Fiji** 名 フィジー《国名》
- **final** 形 最後の
- **financial** 形 財務(上)の
- **find out** 気がつく, 知る
- **Firefox** 名 ファイアフォックス《Mozilla Foundationが開発するウェブブラウザ》
- **firm** 名 会社
- **first** 熟 for the first time 初めて in the first place 最初に love at first sight 一目ぼれ
- **firstly** 副 まず第一に

- ☐ **fit into** ～に収まる
- ☐ **Flight Simulator** フライト・シミュレーター《マイクロソフトが開発していた飛行シミュレーションソフト》
- ☐ **flourish** 動 繁栄する
- ☐ **flow** 名 流れ
- ☐ **fluid** 形 流動的な
- ☐ **fly to** ～まで飛行機で行く
- ☐ **focus** 名 焦点, 関心の的 動 (関心・注意を)集中させる
- ☐ **folder** 名 フォルダ
- ☐ **football** 名 (米国で)アメリカンフットボール
- ☐ **for oneself** 独力で, 自分のために
- ☐ **forbid** 動 禁じる
- ☐ **forbidden** 動 forbid (禁じる)の過去分詞
- ☐ **force** 動 強制する, 余儀なく～させる
- ☐ **forcefully** 副 強力に
- ☐ **forecast** 動 予測する
- ☐ **foresee** 動 予見する
- ☐ **form** 名 記入用紙 動 組織する
- ☐ **format** 名 形式, フォーマット
- ☐ **forth** 副 前へ back and forth 前後に
- ☐ **fortune** 名 財産
- ☐ **forum** 名 公開討論
- ☐ **foundation** 名 財団法人, 基金
- ☐ **founder** 名 創立者, 設立者
- ☐ **free spirit** 自由な精神の持ち主
- ☐ **freedom** 名 自由
- ☐ **friendly** 形 親しみのある, 友好的な
- ☐ **Friends** 名 『フレンズ』《アメリカの人気青春TVドラマ (1994-2004)》
- ☐ **from ～ to** ～から…まで
- ☐ **"From those to whom much is given, much is expected."** 「多くを与えられた人は, 多くのことを期待される」
- ☐ **full-time** 名 常勤の

- ☐ **fun** 熟 make fun of ～を物笑いの種にする, からかう
- ☐ **fund** 動 資金を出す
- ☐ **funeral** 名 葬儀
- ☐ **funnily enough** おかしな話だが
- ☐ **furiously** 副 猛烈に
- ☐ **furnished** 形 家具付きの
- ☐ **future** 熟 in the future 将来において
- ☐ **futurist** 名 未来派の人
- ☐ **futurologist** 名 未来学者

G

- ☐ **gaming** 名 ゲーム 形 ゲーム用の
- ☐ **gang** 名 暴力団, ギャング drug gang 麻薬密売人
- ☐ **gap** 名 隔たり
- ☐ **Gary Kildall** ゲイリー・キルドール《人名》
- ☐ **gas** 名 ガソリン
- ☐ **geek** 名 オタク, マニア
- ☐ **General Electric** ゼネラル・エレクトリック《社名》
- ☐ **generally** 副 概して
- ☐ **generate** 動 生み出す
- ☐ **genius** 名 天才
- ☐ **gentle** 形 温和な
- ☐ **George Lucas** ジョージ・ルーカス《米国の映画監督》
- ☐ **get** 熟 get a job 職を得る get back 戻る, 帰る get behind 後れを取る get better (病気などが)良くなる get into ～に入る get on (乗り物などに)乗る get rich 金持ちになる get sick 病気になる get smaller 小さくなる get to know 知るようになる, 知り合う get worse 悪化する
- ☐ **gifted** 形 才能のある
- ☐ **ginger ale** ジンジャーエール

Word List

- **girlfriend** 名 彼女, ガールフレンド
- **give away** ただで与える, 贈る
- **give up** あきらめる, やめる
- **Giving Pledge** 寄付誓約宣言, ギビング・プレッジ《寄付啓蒙活動》
- **global** 形 世界的な, 国際的な
- **globally** 副 世界規模で
- **go** 熟 go and ~しに行く go away 立ち去る go back to ~に帰る[戻る] go down a road 道を進む go for ~を追い求める, ~を好む go into ~に入る, (仕事)に就く go on to ~に移る, ~に取り掛かる go out 外出する go out with 交際する, 付き合う
- **golf** 名 ゴルフ
- **good** 熟 be not good for ~に良くない
- **goods** 名 商品 consumer goods 消費財
- **Google** 名 グーグル《社名, 同社の検索エンジン》
- **government** 名 政府
- **grade** 名 学年 動 格付けする
- **gradually** 副 だんだんと
- **graduate** 動 卒業する
- **graph** 名 図表, グラフ
- **graphic** 名 図形, 絵
- **graphical** 形 グラフィックの graphical user interface グラフィカル・ユーザー・インターフェース《操作対象が図で表現され, 直感的に操作できる画面表示様式》
- **grid** 名 配線網, 送電系統 electrical grid 配電網
- **grow into [to]** (成長して) ~になる
- **grown-up** 名 大人
- **guest** 名 客, ゲスト
- **GUI** 略 グラフィカル・ユーザー・インターフェース (= graphical user interface)《操作対象が図で表現され, 直感的に操作できる画面表示様式》
- **guitar** 名 ギター
- **guru** 名 教祖的存在, 第一人者
- **guy** 名 男, やつ

H

- **hack** 動 (コンピューターシステムに) 不正侵入する
- **halfway through** ~の途中で
- **handle** 動 取り扱う
- **hard to** ~し難い
- **hardcore** 形 本格的な, 筋金入りの
- **hardware** 名 (コンピューターの) ハードウェア
- **Harry Potter** ハリー・ポッター《架空のキャラクター, 魔法使い》
- **Harvard** 名 ハーバード大学
- **Harvard Square** ハーバードスクエア《米国の地名》
- **hate** 動 嫌う, 憎む
- **Hawaii** 名 ハワイ《米国の州》
- **headline** 名 (新聞などの) 見出し
- **headmaster** 名 (小・中学校の) 校長
- **hear of** ~について聞く[耳にする]
- **heating** 名 暖房 (装置)
- **heavily** 副 ひどく
- **helicopter** 名 ヘリコプター
- **help with** ~を手伝う
- **help ~ to** ~が…するのを助ける
- **helpful** 形 役に立つ
- **here are** ~がある, ~を以下に列挙する
- **Hewlett Packard** ヒューレット・パッカード《社名》
- **hey** 間 おい, ちょっと
- **higher-end** 形 最高級の
- **highly** 副 高く評価して
- **highway** 名 幹線道路

THE BILL GATES STORY

- **hire** 動 雇う, 賃借りする
- **HIV** 略 ヒト免疫不全ウィルス, エイズウィルス (= human immunodeficiency virus)
- **hobbyist** 名 (熱烈な)愛好家
- **hold back** 自制する
- **home** 熟 at home 自宅で
- **Homebrew Computer Club** ホームブリュー・コンピューター・クラブ《コンピューター同好会》
- **homeless** 形 家のない, ホームレスの
- **honestly** 副 正直に
- **honeymoon** 名 新婚旅行
- **Honeywell** 名 ハネウェル《社名》
- **honor** 名 名誉
- **honorary doctorate** 名誉博士号
- **Hood Canal** フッドカナル《アメリカの地名》
- **host** 名 (テレビなどの)司会者 動 司会をする
- **household** 形 家族の
- **how to** ~する方法
- **however** 接 けれども, だが
- **huge** 形 巨大な, ばく大な
- **hyphen** 名 ハイフン, -

I

- **IBM** 略 IBM《社名, = International Business Machines Corporation》
- **identify** 動 (正体などを)割り出す, 見分ける
- **if** 熟 as if あたかも~のように, まるで~みたいに even if たとえ~でも what if もし~だったらどうなるだろうか
- **ignore** 動 無視する, 怠る
- **Illinois** 名 イリノイ州, イリノイ大学
- **image** 名 印象
- **imagine** 動 想像する
- **immediately** 副 すぐに
- **immunization** 名 予防接種
- **impairment** 名 損害
- **impatient** 形 性急な, イライラした
- **import** 動 輸入する
- **importance** 名 重要性
- **importantly** 副 重要なことには
- **impotence** 名 無気力, 性的不能
- **impress** 動 印象づける
- **impression** 名 印象
- **Inc.** 略 有限(責任)会社(= incorporated)
- **include** 動 ~を含める, 盛り込む
- **including** 前 ~を含めて
- **increasingly** 副 ますます
- **incredible** 形 すばらしい, とてつもない
- **indeed** 副 本当に
- **independent** 形 独立した
- **Indian** 名 インド人
- **industry** 名 産業, 工業
- **inequality** 名 不平等
- **inequity** 名 不公平
- **influence** 名 影響 動 影響をおよぼす
- **influential** 形 影響力の大きい
- **Information Systems Incorporated** インフォメーション・システムズ社《社名》
- **in-house** 形 社内の
- **inspire** 動 鼓舞する
- **install** 動 (ソフトなどを)インストールする
- **instance** 熟 for instance たとえば
- **instead** 副 その代わりに instead of ~の代わりに, ~をしないで

Word List

- **instruction** 名 指示
- **Intel** 名 インテル《社名, 同社が開発するマイクロプロセッサの名称》
- **intellectual** 名 有識者
- **intelligent** 形 聡明な
- **intense** 形 (感情などが) 強烈な, 激しい
- **intensity** 名 強烈さ
- **intensively** 副 徹底的に
- **interface** 名 インターフェース《異なる機械同士や機械と人間の接続をする部分》
- **Internet Explorer** インターネット・エクスプローラー《マイクロソフトのウェブブラウザ》
- **Internet-compatible** 形 インターネット対応の
- **internship** 名 実習生, インターンシップ
- **interpreter** 名 通訳, 解釈プログラム
- **intuition** 名 直感, 洞察
- **invaluable** 形 とても有益な
- **invent** 動 発明[考案]する
- **invest** 動 投資する
- **investigate** 動 調査する, 捜査する
- **investment** 名 投資, 出資
- **investor** 名 投資家
- **involve** 動 ～と関わる
- **iOS** 名 アイオーエス《アップル社のモバイルOS》
- **iPad** 名 アイパッド《アップル社のタブレット型PC》
- **iPhone** 名 アイフォン《アップル社のスマートフォン》
- **iPod** 名 アイポッド《アップル社の携帯型音楽プレイヤー》
- **ironically** 副 皮肉にも
- **issue** 名 問題
- **It is ～ for someone to** (人)が…するのは～だ
- **itself** 代 それ自体, それ自身
- **Ivy League** アイビーリーグ《米国北東部の名門8大学の総称》

J

- **J.P. Morgan** ジョン・ピアポント・モルガン《銀行家, 1837-1913》
- **Jack Sams** ジャック・サムズ《人名》
- **jacket** 名 短い上着
- **James Bond** ジェイムズ・ボンド《架空のキャラクター, 英国の秘密諜報員》
- **James Dole** ジェームズ・ドール《人名》
- **Jay Leno** ジェイ・レノ《人名》
- **Jennifer Aniston** ジェニファー・アニストン《人名》
- **jet** 名 ジェット機
- **jewelry** 名 宝飾品類
- **Jewish** 形 ユダヤ人の
- **Jim Clark** ジム・クラーム《人名》
- **Jimi Hendrix** ジミ・ヘンドリックス《アメリカのギタリスト》
- **job** 熟 get a job 職を得る
- **Johannes Gutenberg** ヨハネス・グーテンベルク《活版印刷の発明者, 1398-1468》
- **John D. Rockefeller** ジョン・D・ロックフェラー《アメリカの実業家, 慈善家, 1839-1937》
- **John R. Opel** ジョン・R・オペル《人名》
- **joint** 形 共同の
- **joke** 動 冗談を言う
- **journalist** 名 報道関係者, ジャーナリスト
- **judge** 名 裁判官, 判事
- **junk food** ジャンクフード
- **just as** ～と同程度に

THE BILL GATES STORY

K

- **Katherine Graham** キャサリン・グラハム《人名》
- **kB** 略 キロバイト(= kilobyte)《情報量の大きさを表す単位》
- **keep on ~[-ing]** ～し続ける
- **keep track of** ～の記録をつける
- **keep someone from** ～から(人)を阻む
- **keyboard** 名 キーボード
- **killer** 名 殺し屋
- **kilometer** 名 キロメートル《長さの単位》
- **kit** 名 道具一式
- **know** 熟 get to know 知るようになる, 知り合う
- **know-how** 名 ノウハウ
- **knowledge** 名 知識
- **Kristianne Gates** クリスティーネ・ゲイツ《人名》

L

- **lack** 名 不足
- **Lakeside School** レイクサイドスクール《私立学校》
- **Lanai** 名 ラナイ島《アメリカ・ハワイ州の地名》
- **laptop** 名 ノート型パソコン
- **Las Vegas** ラスベガス《アメリカの地名》
- **latest** 形 最新の
- **launch** 動 (事業などを)始める, (新商品を)発売する 名 (事業などの)開始
- **lawsuit** 名 訴訟
- **lawyer** 名 弁護士
- **lazy** 形 怠惰な, 無精な
- **lead to** ～に至る, ～を引き起こす
- **leadership** 名 指揮
- **leave** 熟 be left behind 後れを取る take a leave of absence 休学する
- **led** 動 lead (導く)の過去, 過去分詞
- **LED** 略 発光ダイオード(= light-emitting diode)
- **left behind** 《be –》後れを取る
- **left-wing** 名 左派, 急進派
- **legal** 形 法律(上)の
- **Leonardo da Vinci** レオナルド・ダ・ヴィンチ《芸術家, 1452-1519》
- **less** 形 ～より小さい[少ない] 副 ～より少なく, ～ほどでなく
- **level** 名 水準
- **license** 名 (使用権などの)許諾 動 使用権を認める
- **lie** 動 うそをつく
- **lifesaving** 形 救命の
- **lifetime** 名 生涯
- **lift ~ out of** ～を…からすくい上げる
- **light up** 点灯する
- **lighting** 名 照明
- **like** 熟 look like ～のように見える, ～に似ている sound like ～のように聞こえる
- **limit** 動 限定する
- **link** 名 因果関係
- **Linkedin** 名 リンクトイン《ビジネス用SNS》
- **Linux Foundation** リナックス・ファウンデーション《リナックスの管理事業を行う非営利組織》
- **Lisa** 名 リサ《アップル社のオフィス向けPC》
- **list** 名 一覧表 動 名簿に記入する
- **lit** 動 light (照らす)の過去, 過去分詞
- **literary** 形 文学の
- **London** ロンドン《英国の首都》
- **lonely** 形 孤独な
- **long** 熟 for long 長い間

Word List

- **longer** 熟 no longer もはや〜でない［〜しない］
- **long-sighted** 形 先見の明のある
- **long-term** 形 長期の
- **look like** 〜のように見える、〜に似ている
- **look through** 〜をのぞき込む
- **lose out to** 〜に座を奪われる
- **lose track of** 〜が分からなくなる
- **loser** 名 敗者
- **loss** 名 減少
- **lot of** 《a–》たくさんの〜
- **lots of** たくさんの〜
- **Lotus 1-2-3** ロータス・ワンツースリー《PC用表計算ソフト》
- **love at first sight** 一目ぼれ
- **lower** 形 より低い
- **lowly** 形 地位の低い
- **luxurious** 形 豪華な
- **lying** 動 lie（うそをつく）の現在分詞

M

- **Mac** 略 マック（= Macintosh）《アップル社のPC》
- **Macintosh** 名 マッキントッシュ《アップル社のPC》
- **Macworld** 名 マックワールド《アップル製品の発表・展示会》
- **main** 形 中心的な、主要な
- **mainframe** 名 中央処理装置、（端末に対しての）本体
- **mainly** 副 主に
- **major** 形 大きい、重要な 名 専攻科目
- **make** 熟 make a speech 演説をする make fun of 〜を物笑いの種にする、からかう make it possible for 〜 to … 〜が…できるようにする make money お金を儲ける make sure 確かめる、確認する make up one's mind 決心する
- **maker** 名 製造業者、メーカー
- **malaria** 名 マラリア《伝染病》
- **malnutrition** 名 栄養失調
- **manage** 動 ①動かす、うまく処理する ②経営［管理］する
- **management** 名 経営、管理
- **manager** 名 経営者、部長
- **Manele Bay Hotel** マネレ・ベイ・ホテル
- **man-machine** 形 マンマシンの、人間と機械の間の
- **mansion** 名 大邸宅
- **manual** 名 マニュアル、取り扱い説明書
- **manufacture** 動 製作する
- **manufacturer** 名 製造業者、メーカー
- **manuscript** 名 原稿
- **Marc Andreesen** マーク・アンドリーセン《人名》
- **mark** 熟 as a mark of respect 敬意を表して
- **Mark Zuckerberg** マーク・ザッカーバーグ《人名》
- **market-driven** 形 市場主導の
- **marketing** 名 市場調査、マーケティング
- **marriage** 名 結婚
- **marry** 動 結婚する
- **Mary Gates** メアリー・ゲイツ《人名》
- **massive** 形 巨大な
- **massively** 副 大規模に、飛躍的に
- **master** 名 師匠、マスター 動 修得する
- **match** 動 ぴったり合わせる
- **mathematics** 名 数学
- **Matthew Perry** マシュー・ペリー《人名》

THE BILL GATES STORY

- **Maui** 名 マウイ島《アメリカ・ハワイ州の地名》
- **MBA** 略 経営学修士 (= Master in Business Administration)
- **meanwhile** 副 一方では
- **measure** 名 基準
- **medal** 名 勲章, メダル
- **media** 名 マスコミ, メディア
- **medical** 形 医学の
- **Melinda French (Gates)** メリンダ・フレンチ (ゲイツ)《人名》
- **memo** 名 覚え書き, メモ
- **memorize** 動 暗記する
- **memory** 名 (コンピューターの) メモリ, 記憶装置
- **mention** 動 (〜について) 述べる, 言及する
- **menu** 名 一覧, メニュー
- **merciless** 形 無慈悲な
- **mercy** 名 情け
- **merge** 動 合併する [させる]
- **metric** 名 測定基準
- **Mexico** 名 メキシコ《国名》
- **Micro Instrumentation and Telemetry Systems** マイクロ・インスツルメント&テレメトリー・システム社《社名》
- **microcomputer** 名 超小型コンピューター
- **microprocessor** 名 超小型演算装置, マイクロプロセッサ
- **Microsoft** 名 マイクロソフト《社名》
- **mid** 形 中頃の
- **middle** 名 中頃 形 真ん中の
- **midnight** 名 夜の12時
- **midst** 名 真ん中
- **milestone** 名 (歴史などの) 節目, 一里塚
- **military** 形 軍事の
- **millennium** 名 千年, 西暦2000年
- **millionaire** 名 百万長者, 大金持ち
- **mind** 名 心, 考え make up one's mind 決心する
- **minicomputer** 名 小型コンピューター
- **minority** 名 少数派の
- **mislead** 動 (間違った情報を与えて) あざむく
- **miss out** (チャンスなどを) 逃す, 取りそこなう
- **mission** 名 使命
- **MITS** 略 ミッツ (= Micro Instrumentation and Telemetry Systems)《社名》
- **MMOG** 略 多人数同時参加型オンラインゲーム (= massively multiplayer online game)
- **mobile** 名 携帯電話
- **mode** 名 方式, モード
- **modern** 形 現代の
- **modify** 動 修正する
- **money** 熟 make money お金を儲ける
- **monitor** 名 ディスプレイ, モニタ
- **monopolist** 名 独占者
- **monopoly** 名 ①独占, 独占事業 ②《M-》モノポリー《ボードゲーム》
- **Monte Davidoff** モンティ・ダビドフ《人名》
- **Montreal** 名 モントリオール《カナダの地名》
- **MOOC** 略 大規模公開オンライン講座 (= massive open online course)
- **more** more and more ますます more than 〜以上
- **Mosaic** 名 モザイク《ウェブブラウザ》
- **mostly** 副 多くは, ほとんど
- **motel** 名 モーテル
- **motivate** 動 刺激する
- **motorist** 名 自動車運転者

Word List

- **mouse** 名 (コンピューターの)マウス
- **move around** あちこち移動する
- **move to** ～に引っ越す[移転する]
- **MS-DOS** 略 エムエスドス (= Microsoft Disk Operating System)《パソコン用OS》
- **much** 熟 too much of あまりに～過ぎる
- **multimedia** 名 マルチメディア
- **multiplatform** 形 複数のプラットフォームに対応の
- **multiplayer** 形 (ゲームなどが)多人数参加型の
- **multiple** 形 多数の
- **multitask** 動 同時に複数の仕事をする
- **museum** 名 博物館, 美術館

N

- **naked** 形 裸の
- **name** 熟 name after ～にちなんで名付ける
- **Napoleon** 名 ナポレオン(・ボナパルト)《フランスの軍人, 政治家, 1769–1821》
- **narrow-band** 形 狭帯域の
- **NASDAQ Exchange** ナスダック市場《アメリカのベンチャー向け株式市場》
- **nasty** 形 いやな, 意地の悪い
- **Nathan Myhrvold** ネイサン・ミアボルド《人名》
- **National Center for Supercomputing Applications** 米国立スーパーコンピューター応用研究所
- **nationwide** 形 全国的な
- **NCSA** 略 米国立スーパーコンピューター応用研究所 (= National Center for Supercomputing Applications)
- **nearby** 形 近くの
- **nearly** 副 ほとんど
- **necessary** 形 必要な
- **need to do** ～する必要がある
- **negative** 形 否定的な, マイナスの
- **negotiate** 動 交渉[協議]する
- **neither A nor B** AもBもない
- **nervous** 形 神経質な, やきもきした
- **net asset** 純資産
- **Netflix** 名 ネットフリックス《社名》
- **Netscape Communications** ネットスケープコミュニケーションズ《社名》
- **Netscape Navigator** ネットスケープ・ナビゲーター《ウェブブラウザ》
- **nevertheless** 副 それにもかかわらず
- **New Mexico** ニューメキシコ《米国の州》
- **New York** ニューヨーク《米国の都市;州》
- **New York Palace Hotel** ニューヨークパレスホテル
- **New Zealand** 名 ニュージーランド《国名》
- **news** 名 報道, ニュース
- **newsletter** 名 会報, ニュースレター
- **newspaper** 名 新聞(紙)
- **next-generation** 形 次世代の
- **nickname** 名 あだ名
- **night** 熟 day and night 昼も夜も
- **nightclub** 名 ナイトクラブ
- **no one** 誰も[一人も]～ない
- **nobody** 代 誰も[1人も]～ない
- **Nokia** 名 ノキア《社名》
- **non-disclosure** 形 秘密保持の
- **none** 代 (～の)何も[誰も・少しも]…ない

- **nonetheless** 副 それにもかかわらず
- **non-exclusive** 形 非独占的な
- **non-military** 形 文民の
- **non-student** 名 非学生
- **nor** 接 ～もまたない neither A nor B A も B もない
- **normal** 形 普通の, 平均的な 名 標準
- **note** 名 メモ, 覚え書き
- **nothing** 熟 for nothing ただで, 無料で
- **notice** 動 気づく
- **notion** 名 観念, 概念
- **nourish** 動 栄養を与える
- **now** 熟 right now 目下のところ
- **number of** 《a-》多くの～

O

- **obituary** 名 追悼記事, 訃報
- **object** 動 異議を唱える
- **observation tower** 名 展望塔
- **of course** もちろん, 当然
- **off** 熟 on and off 断続的に
- **offer** 動 申し出る, 提供する
- **officially** 副 正式に
- **oil well** 名 油井
- **okay** 形 よい, 大丈夫で
- **Olympic Mountains** オリンピック山脈
- **Omaha** 名 オマハ《アメリカの地名》
- **on and off** 断続的に
- **one** 熟 no one 誰も [一人も] ～ない one day (過去の) ある日, (未来の) いつか one of ～の1つ [人]
- **online** 名 オンライン 形 オンラインの, ネットワーク上の
- **open source** オープン・ソース《公開されていて自由に利用・変更ができるソース》
- **open-architecture** 名 オープン・アーキテクチャ《ハードやソフトの仕様を一般公開して, 誰もがそれに準じた製品を作れるようにすること》
- **operating systen** オペレーティング・システム《コンピューター操作の中心となるソフトウェア》
- **opportunity** 名 好機
- **opposite** 名 反対の人 [物]
- **optimist** 名 楽天家
- **optimistic** 形 楽観的な
- **option** 名 選択 (の余地)
- **ordinary** 形 普通の
- **organization** 名 組織, 団体
- **origin** 名 起源
- **original** 形 始めの, 元の
- **originally** 副 元は
- **OS** 略 オーエス, オペレーティング・システム (= operating systen)《コンピューター操作の中心となるソフトウェア》
- **OS/2** 名 オーエスツー《IBM・マイクロソフト共同開発の OS》
- **other** 熟 in other words すなわち, 言い換えれば
- **out of** ①～から外へ, ～から抜け出して ②～から作り出して, ～を材料として ③～の範囲外に, ～から離れて ④(ある数) の中から one out of ten 10のうち 1, 1 割
- **outdated** 形 時代遅れの
- **outline** 動 ～の要点を述べる
- **outperform** 動 ～をしのぐ
- **output** 名 生産
- **overall** 形 全体の
- **overhear** 動 ふと耳にする
- **overheard** 動 overhear (ふと耳にする) の過去, 過去分詞
- **overlap** 動 ～を重ね合わせる
- **overlook** 動 見渡す

Word List

- **over-powerful** 形 すさまじい
- **owe** 動 〜を支払う義務がある
- **own** 熟 of one's own 自分自身の
- **owner** 名 持ち主, オーナー

P

- **P&G** 名 ピーアンドジー《社名》
- **pace** 動 行ったり来たりする
- **paid** 動 pay（払う）の過去, 過去分詞
- **palace** 名 宮殿
- **panel** 名 計器盤, パネル
- **paragraph** 名 段落
- **parallel** 形 類似の, 同様の
- **PARC** 略 パロアルト研究所 (= Palo Alto Research Center)《ゼロックス社が開設した研究開発企業》
- **parent** 名 〈-s〉両親
- **part** 熟 play a part 役目を果たす take part in 〜に参加する
- **partly** 副 一部分は, ある程度は
- **partner** 名 仲間, 同僚 動 (〜と)組む
- **partnership** 名 提携, パートナーシップ
- **password** 名 パスワード
- **Paul Allen** 名 ポール・アレン《人名》
- **pay** 動 支払う 名 給料
- **payroll** 名 給料支払簿
- **PC** 略 パソコン (= personal computer)
- **PC/AT** 略 ピーシーエーティー《IBMのPC》
- **PC-DOS** 略 ピーシードス《IBMとマイクロソフト共同開発のOS》
- **pdf** 略 ピーディーエフ (= portable document format)
- **Penguin Group** ペンギン・グループ《社名》
- **per** 前 〜につき, 〜ごとに
- **percentage** 名 割合, 比率
- **performance** 名 成績, 業績
- **perhaps** 副 たぶん, ことによると
- **period** 名 期間
- **personal** 形 個人の
- **persuade** 動 説得する
- **pharmaceutical** 形 薬剤の
- **philanthropic** 形 慈善の, 人道主義の
- **philanthropist** 名 慈善家
- **philanthropy** 名 慈善活動, 社会奉仕事業
- **Philippe Kahn** フィリップ・カーン《人名》
- **Phoebe Gates** フィービー・ゲイツ《人名》
- **photo** 名 写真
- **photographer** 名 写真家, カメラマン
- **phrase** 名 句, フレーズ
- **picture** 熟 take a picture 写真を撮る
- **pier** 名 桟橋
- **pin** 名 細い留め具, ピン
- **pineapple** 名 パイナップル
- **pioneer** 名 開拓者, 先駆者
- **piracy** 名 著作権侵害, 海賊行為
- **pitiless** 形 無慈悲な
- **place** 熟 in the first place 最初に take place 行われる
- **plan to do** 〜するつもりである
- **plantation** 名 大農園
- **play a part** 役目を果たす
- **play along with** 〜に合わせて演奏する
- **player** 名 再生機, プレイヤー
- **plenty of** たくさんの〜
- **pneumonia** 名 肺炎
- **pocket-sized** 形 ポケットサイズ

- の
- **point of view** 考え方, 視点
- **point out** 指摘する
- **poker** 名 ポーカー《トランプのゲーム》
- **policy** 名 政策, 方針
- **polio** 名 小児まひ
- **political** 形 政治の
- **politician** 名 政治家
- **Pong** 名 ポン《卓球ゲーム》
- **pool** 名 プール
- **Popular Electronics** ポピュラー・エレクトロニクス《雑誌》
- **popularity** 名 人気, 流行
- **Portland** 名 ポートランド《アメリカの地名》
- **position** 名 立場, 状況
- **possible** 形 ①可能な ②ありうる, 起こりうる as ~ as possible できるだけ~ make it possible for ~ to ~が…できるようにする
- **potential** 名 可能性, 潜在能力
- **pour** 動 注ぐ
- **poverty** 名 貧困
- **powerful** 形 力強い, 実力のある, 影響力のある
- **PowerPoint** 名 パワーポイント《マイクロソフトのプレゼンテーションソフト》
- **practical** 形 実際的な, 実用的な
- **predict** 動 予測[予想]する
- **prefer** 動 (~のほうを)好む
- **preference** 名 好み
- **pre-law** 形 法学部入学準備の
- **prep school** 高校, 予備校
- **preparation** 名 準備, 心構え
- **prepare for** ~の準備をする
- **presence** 名 存在(感)
- **presentation** 名 発表, プレゼンテーション
- **president** 名 ①大統領 ②社長
- **Presidential Medal of Freedom** 大統領自由勲章
- **press** 名 報道陣, マスコミ press conference 記者会見
- **pressure** 名 圧力, プレッシャー put pressure on ~に圧力をかける
- **pretend** 動 ふりをする, 装う
- **prevent** 動 妨げる
- **price** 名 ①値段 ②〈-s〉相場
- **Princeton** 名 プリンストン《地名》, プリンストン大学
- **printer** 名 印刷機, プリンター
- **printing** 名 印刷
- **priority** 名 優先[順位]
- **privacy** 名 (干渉されない)自由な生活, プライバシー
- **private** 形 ①私的な, 個人の ②民間の, 私立の
- **privately** 副 個人的に
- **probably** 副 たぶん
- **processor** 名 中央演算処理装置, プロセッサ
- **product** 名 製品
- **profession** 名 専門職
- **profit** 名 利益
- **programmer** 名 プログラマー
- **programming** 名 プログラミング
- **progress** 動 進展する
- **project** 名 計画, プロジェクト
- **promote** 動 ①宣伝する ②昇進させる
- **promotion** 名 ①宣伝販売 ②促進
- **property** 名 所有地
- **propose** 動 ①提案する ②結婚を申し込む
- **prostitute** 名 売春婦
- **proud** 形 自慢の be proud of ~を自慢に思う

Word List

- **proven** 形 実績のある
- **provide** 動 供給する, 用意する
- **provider** 名 インターネット接続業者, プロバイダー
- **PS/2** 名 ピーエスツー《IBMのPCシリーズ》
- **psychology** 名 心理学
- **public** 形 公共の, 公開の in public 公の場で take ~ publice ~を上場する
- **publish** 動 ①公表する ②発行する
- **publisher** 名 出版社
- **pull-down** 形 プルダウンの, ドロップダウンの
- **punch** 動 (穴あけパンチで)穴を開ける
- **push down** 押し下げる
- **put ~ in** ~を…の中に入れる
- **put pressure on** ~に圧力をかける
- **put up** ~を上げる

Q

- **quality** 名 品質
- **quarter** 名 4分の1
- **quickly** 副 すぐに
- **Quicktime** 名 クイックタイム《アップル社のマルチメディア・ソフトウェア》
- **quit** 動 辞職する
- **quite a few** かなり多くの

R

- **racquetball** 名 ラケットボール
- **raise** 動 (数量を)上げる
- **Ralph Nader** ラルフ・ネーダー《人名》
- **ranking** 名 順位, ランキング
- **rare** 形 まれな
- **rather** 副 ①むしろ, かえって ②かなり, やや rather than ~よりむしろ
- **ready to** 《be – 》すぐに~できる, ~する用意がある
- **real-estate** 名 不動産
- **realize** 動 ~に気づく, ~を悟る
- **recently** 副 最近
- **reception** 名 受付
- **recognition** 名 認証
- **recognize** 動 認識する
- **record** 名 記録
- **recovery** 名 回復
- **reduce** 動 減じる
- **reduction** 名 減少
- **Reed Hastings** リード・ヘイスティングス《人名》
- **refer to** ~に言及する
- **reflect** 動 反映する
- **refrigerator** 名 冷蔵庫
- **refugee** 名 難民
- **refuse** 動 拒絶する
- **regard** 動 (~を…と)見なす
- **rehire** 動 ~を再雇用する
- **relationship** 名 関係
- **relax** 動 くつろぐ, リラックスする
- **release** 動 公開する, 発売する 名 公開
- **remarkable** 形 注目に値する
- **remote** 形 遠い, 遠隔の
- **repackage** 動 修正変更して再リリースする
- **replace** 動 ~に取って代わる
- **reply** 動 答える, 返事をする 名 返事
- **representative** 名 代表(者)
- **reputation** 名 評判
- **rescue** 動 救う

- **research** 名 調査, 研究
- **researcher** 名 研究者
- **resign** 動 辞職する
- **resort** 名 行楽地, リゾート
- **respect** 名 尊敬 動 尊敬する as a mark of respect 敬意を表して
- **respond** 動 反応する
- **response** 名 反応, 返答
- **responsible** 形 責任のある
- **result** 名 結果, 成り行き, 成績 as a result その結果(として)
- **revenue** 名 収入, 利益
- **review** 名 ①書評, 評論 ②審査
- **reviewer** 名 評論家
- **revise** 動 改訂する
- **revolution** 名 革命
- **rich** 熟 get rich 金持ちになる
- **right now** 目下のところ
- **right-hand** 形 最も頼りになる
- **rigid** 形 融通のきかない
- **ring** 名 指輪
- **Risk** 名 リスク《ボードゲーム》
- **Robert Redford** ロバート・レッドフォード《アメリカの俳優, 映画監督, 1936–》
- **rock back and forth** 前後に揺らす
- **role** 名 役割 take on the role of ~ の役割を引き受ける
- **roll** 名 (紙などの)一巻き
- **Rolling Stones** ローリング・ストーンズ《イギリスのロックバンド》
- **roof** 名 天井
- **roommate** 名 ルームメイト, 部屋を共有する相手
- **Rory Gates** ローリー・ゲイツ《人名》
- **rotate** 動 回転する
- **roughly** 副 おおよそ
- **rude** 形 失礼な
- **rummage sale** 慈善バザー
- **run over to** ~へ急いでやってくる

S

- **sadly** 副 不幸にも
- **saint** 名 聖人
- **salary** 名 給料
- **sale** 熟 rummage sale 慈善バザー
- **sand** 名 砂
- **sarcastically** 副 皮肉を込めて
- **SAT** 名 大学進学適性試験(= Scholastic Assessment Test)
- **satisfied with**《be –》~に満足する
- **Satya Nadella** サティア・ナデラ《人名》
- **saying** 名 ことわざ, 格言
- **schedule** 名 予定, スケジュール 動 予定を立てる
- **scholar** 名 学生, 奨学生
- **schoolteacher** 名 学校の教師
- **score** 名 成績, スコア
- **screen** 名 画面
- **sea change** 大転換, 様変わり
- **search engine** 検索ソフト, サーチ・エンジン
- **Seattle** 名 シアトル《アメリカの地名》
- **Seattle Computer Products** シアトル・コンピューター・プロダクツ《社名》
- **second-generation** 形 第二世代の
- **secondly** 副 第2に, 次に
- **secretly** 副 内緒で
- **security** 名 ①警備, セキュリティー ②安全保障 social security contributions 社会保険負担
- **seem** 動 (~に)見える, (~のよう

- に)思われる
- **seen as** 《be –》~として見られる
- **semester** 名 (前期・後期の)学期
- **send out** 送信する
- **senior** 形 ①年長者 ②《S–》~・シニア《姓名のあとにつけて親であることを表す》
- **sense** 名 感じ 動 感じる, 気づく
- **sensor** 名 感知装置, センサー
- **separate** 動 分ける
- **serious** 形 重大な, 深刻な
- **seriously** 副 真剣に, 重大に
- **service** 名 業務, サービス
- **set up** 設立する, 組み立てる
- **shareholder** 名 株主
- **shift** 動 代える
- **Shirley Temple** シャーリー・テンプル《ノンアルコールカクテル》
- **shit** 名 くだらないこと, たちの悪い非難
- **shocked** 形 ~にショックを受けて, 憤慨して
- **shoot up** 急上昇する
- **short** 熟 in short 手短に言えば
- **shortly** 副 まもなく
- **shut down** 停止する
- **shy** 形 内気な, 恥ずかしがりの
- **sick** 熟 get sick 病気になる
- **sight** 熟 love at first sight 一目ぼれ
- **significant** 形 大幅な
- **Silicon Valley** シリコンバレー《地名》
- **similar** 形 同じような
- **simulator** 名 擬似実験装置, シミュレーター Flight Simulator フライトシミュレーター《マイクロソフトが開発していた飛行シミュレーションソフト》
- **since** 熟 ever since それ以来ずっと

- **singer** 名 歌手
- **Singing in the Rain** 『雨に唄えば』《アメリカ映画》
- **single** 形 たった1つの
- **Siri** 名 シリ《アップル社の秘書機能アプリ》
- **sit-on-the-beach** 形 海辺でぼんやりする
- **skiing** 名 スキー water skiing 水上スキー
- **skill** 名 技能
- **skilled** 形 熟練した
- **skinny** 形 やせた
- **skip** 動 飛び級する
- **Skype** 名 スカイプ《インターネット電話サービス》
- **slightly** 副 わずかに
- **smaller** 熟 get smaller 小さくなる
- **smart** 形 ①利口な ②洗練された
- **smartphone** 名 スマートフォン
- **so** 熟 and so on ~など, その他もろもろ so that ~するために, ~できるように so ~ that 非常に~なので…
- **sociable** 形 社交的な
- **social** 形 社会の social security contributions 社会保険負担
- **society** 名 社会
- **software** 名 ソフト(ウェア)
- **some time** いつか, そのうち
- **somebody** 代 誰か
- **someone** 代 ある人, 誰か
- **something** 代 何か
- **sometimes** 副 時々
- **somewhere** 副 どこかで
- **Sony** 名 ソニー《社名》
- **soon** 熟 as soon as ~するとすぐ
- **sort of** 《a –》~のようなもの, 一種の~
- **Sound Families Initiative** サウンド・ファミリーズ・イニシアティ

THE BILL GATES STORY

- ブ《慈善事業》
- **sound like** ～のように聞こえる，～のような印象を与える
- **source** 名 ソース，情報源 open source オープン・ソース《公開されていて自由に利用・変更ができるソース》source code ソース・コード
- **Space Needle** スペース・ニードル《展望タワー》
- **Spacewar** 名 スペースウォー《対戦型PCゲーム》
- **speaker** 名 スピーカー
- **spec** 名 仕様書
- **speech** 熟 make a speech 演説をする
- **speed** 名 速度
- **spirit** 名 精神 free spirit 自由な精神の持ち主
- **split into** ～に分かれる
- **split up** 別れる
- **spontaneous** 形 自然な
- **spreadsheet** 名 表計算ソフト，スプレッドシート
- **Spyglass** 名 スパイグラス《社名》
- **square** 名 正方形
- **stacked ranking** スタック・ランキング《人事評価システム》
- **staff** 名 職員，スタッフ
- **stage** 名 ①舞台 ②段階
- **standard** 名 標準，規格
- **Standard Oil** スタンダード・オイル《社名》
- **Stanford** 名 スタンフォード大学
- **start** 熟 start doing ～し始める start to do ～し始める
- **startle** 動 びっくりさせる
- **startup** 名 新規事業
- **state** 名 ①あり様，状態 ②国家，(アメリカなどの) 州
- **statistics** 名 統計(学)
- **stay on** とどまる
- **steal** 盗む
- **steel** 名 鋼，鋼鉄(製の物)
- **Steve Ballmer** スティーブ・バルマー《人名》
- **Steve Jobs** スティーブ・ジョブズ《アメリカの実業家，アップル社創立者, 1955-2011》
- **Steve Mcgregor** スティーブ・マクレガー《人名》
- **Steve Russell** スティーブ・ラッセル《人名》
- **Steve Wozniak** スティーブ・ウォズニアック《人名》
- **stock** 名 株式
- **stole** 動 steal (盗む) の過去
- **stolen** 動 steal (盗む) の過去分詞
- **stop doing** ～するのをやめる
- **strategic** 形 戦略上の
- **strategy** 名 戦略，方針
- **stupid** 形 ばかな
- **style** 名 様式，スタイル
- **subsidiary** 名 関連子会社
- **suburb** 名 近郊
- **succeed** 動 成功する
- **success** 名 成功
- **successful** 形 成功した
- **successfully** 副 首尾よく
- **such a** そのような
- **such as** たとえば～，～のような
- **such ～ that** 非常に～なので…
- **suggest** 動 ①提案する ②示唆する
- **suggestion** 名 提案，忠告
- **suit** 名 背広，スーツ in suits スーツ姿の
- **summon** 動 呼び出す
- **sunset** 名 夕焼け
- **superhighway** 名 高速幹線道路
- **supplier** 名 納入業者
- **support** 名 支援，後押し

Word List

- **supposed to** 《be –》~することになっている, ~するはずである
- **sure** 熟 make sure 確かめる, 確認する
- **surf** 動 ネットサーフィンをする
- **Surface Book** サーフェス・ブック《マイクロソフトのノートPC》
- **surprised at** 《be –》~に驚く
- **survival** 名 生き残ること
- **suspicious** 形 疑い深い
- **swiftly** 副 迅速に
- **switch** 名 スイッチ 動 スイッチを入れる[切る]
- **switchover** 名 切り替え
- **Switzerland** 名 スイス《国名》
- **symbol** 名 象徴, シンボル
- **systematic** 形 計画的な

T

- **table tennis** 卓球
- **tactic** 名 戦術
- **tagline** 名 キャッチフレーズ
- **take** 熟 take a leave of absence 休学する take a picture 写真を撮る take control of ~を制御[支配]する take on ~に挑戦する, (仕事などを)引き受ける take on the role of ~の役割を引き受ける take part in ~に参加する take place 行われる take ~ public ~を上場する take someone out (人を)連れ出す take someone out of (人を) ~から出す take someone to (人を) ~に連れて行く take time off work 仕事を休む take up やり始める take ~ to …するのに(~の時間が)かかる
- **talent** 名 才能
- **tape** 名 テープ, 平ひも
- **taste** 名 好み, 趣味
- **tax** 名 税金
- **taxpayer** 名 納税者
- **TB** 略 結核 (= tuberculosis)
- **tech** 名 科学技術
- **technique** 名 技術
- **technology** 名 科学技術, テクノロジー
- **TED Talks** テッドトーク《動画の無料配信プロジェクト》
- **teenage** 形 10代の, ティーンエイジャーの
- **teenager** 名 10代の人, ティーンエイジャー《13歳から19歳》
- **teleconference** 名 テレビ会議
- **Teletype** 名 テレタイプ《電動タイプライター》
- **television** 名 テレビ
- **tell** 熟 tell ~ to ~に…するように言う
- **Tennessee** 名 テネシー《アメリカの州》
- **tennis** 名 テニス table tennis 卓球
- **tent** 名 天幕, テント
- **terminal** 名 端末装置
- **Texas** 名 テキサス《アメリカの州》
- **text** 名 文字列
- **text-based** 形 テキストベースの, 操作をキーボードで行う
- **than** 熟 more than ~以上 rather than ~よりむしろ
- **thanks to** ~のおかげで, ~の結果
- **That is about all.** (話すことは)それくらいです。
- **theater** 名 劇場
- **then** 形 当時の
- **therapist** 名 療法士, セラピスト
- **these days** このごろ
- **thinker** 名 思索家
- **thirdly** 副 第三に
- **those** 熟 in those days あのころは, 当時は

THE BILL GATES STORY

- ☐ **though** 副 しかし **even though ~** であるけれども、~にもかかわらず
- ☐ **threat** 名 脅威
- ☐ **tic-tac-toe** 名 三目並べ
- ☐ **tidal wave** 大変動
- ☐ **Tim Paterson** ティム・パターソン《人名》
- ☐ **time** 熟 **all the time** いつも、その間ずっと **at the time** そのころ、当時は **at this time** 現時点では、このとき **by the time** ~する時までに **every time** ~するときはいつも **some time** いつか、そのうち **take time off work** 仕事を休む
- ☐ **time-sharing** 形 時間割の、共同使用の
- ☐ **timing** 名 頃合、タイミング
- ☐ **tiny** 形 とても小さい
- ☐ **title** 名 題名、タイトル
- ☐ **total** 形 完全な
- ☐ **tough** 形 骨の折れる、困難な
- ☐ **tour** 名 小旅行、ツアー
- ☐ **tourist** 名 観光客
- ☐ **trace** 動 さかのぼって調べる
- ☐ **track** 名 軌道、跡 **keep track of ~** の記録をつける **lose track of ~** が分からなくなる
- ☐ **tractor** 名 牽引自動車、トラクター
- ☐ **trade-fair** 名 産業見本市
- ☐ **trading** 名 商取引
- ☐ **tradition** 名 伝統
- ☐ **traditional** 形 伝統的な
- ☐ **traffic** 名 交通(量)
- ☐ **Traf-O-Data** 名 トラフ・オー・データ《交通量測定コンピューターとそのプログラム》
- ☐ **trampoline** 名 トランポリン
- ☐ **treat** 動 治療する
- ☐ **treatment** 名 療養
- ☐ **trend** 名 流行、トレンド
- ☐ **trick** 動 だます

- ☐ **trigger** 動 (出来事などを)引き起こす
- ☐ **trouble** 熟 **in trouble** 面倒な状況で、困って
- ☐ **trust** 動 信頼する
- ☐ **tuberculosis** 名 結核
- ☐ **turn into** ~に変わる、~に進路を向ける
- ☐ **turn off** (照明などを)消す
- ☐ **turn out to be** 結局(~であるということが)わかる
- ☐ **turnaround** 名 ターンアラウンド《輸送機などが荷物の積み下ろしと燃料補給などを行って再び出発できるようになるまでの過程》**"turnaround time" of seven hours**《退社から出社までが7時間》
- ☐ **typical** 形 典型的な

U

- ☐ **U.S.** 略 アメリカ (= United States)
- ☐ **U2** 名 ユートゥー《アイルランドのロックバンド》
- ☐ **UCSD Pascal** UCSDパスカル《カリフォルニア大学サンディエゴ校(UCSD)が開発したソフトウェア》
- ☐ **undergraduate degree** 学士号
- ☐ **underground** 形 地下の[にある]
- ☐ **underwater** 形 水中(用)の
- ☐ **unfortunately** 副 不幸にも
- ☐ **unhappy** 形 不幸な
- ☐ **unimaginative** 形 想像力に欠ける
- ☐ **unimportant** 形 ささいな
- ☐ **unit** 名 装置一式
- ☐ **unite** 動 団結する
- ☐ **United States** 名 アメリカ合衆国《国名》
- ☐ **United Way of America** ユナイテッド・ウェイ・オブ・アメリカ《慈

Word List

善福祉団体》
- **university** 名（総合）大学
- **unjust** 形不公平な
- **unlikely** 形ありそうもない
- **unpaid-for** 形未払いの
- **unpleasant** 形不愉快な
- **unprofitable** 形無益な，不採算の
- **unsettling** 形落ち着かない，不安な
- **unusually** 形異常に
- **unveil** 動明らかにする，ベールを取る
- **upbringing** 名しつけ，育て方
- **upper-middle** 形中の上の
- **used to** 以前は～だった，以前はよく～したものだった
- **user** 名使用者，利用者
- **usual** 形いつもの，平常な as usual いつものように，相変わらず

V

- **vaccine** 名ワクチン
- **Valentine's day** バレンタインデー
- **valuable** 形貴重な，価値のある
- **value** 名価値 動評価する，値をつける
- **vaporware** 名ベイパーウェア，いつ出るか分からない霞のようなソフト［ハード］
- **version** 名バージョン，版
- **versus** 前対，～に対して
- **via** 前～経由で，～によって
- **view** 熟 point of view 考え方，視点
- **virtually** 副コンピュータ上で
- **VisiCorp** 名ビジコープ《社名》
- **vision** 名先見，洞察力
- **Visi On** ビジオン《ビジコープのOS》
- **visionary** 名夢想家
- **visitor** 名訪問客
- **volume** 名量，豊富さ

W

- **Waldorf Astoria Hotel** ウォルドルフ＝アストリア《高級ホテルブランド》
- **Wang Laboratories** ワング・ラボラトリーズ《社名》
- **warn** 動警告する
- **Warren Buffett** ウォーレン・バフェット《人名》
- **Washington** 名ワシントン《米国の首都；州》
- **water-skiing** 名水上スキー
- **wave** 名波 tidal wave 大変動
- **way of** ～する方法
- **way to** ～する方法
- **wealth** 名財産
- **web** 名ウェブ（=World Wide Web）
- **website** 名ウェブサイト
- **wedding** 名結婚式，婚礼
- **WEF** 略世界経済協議会（= World Economic Forum）
- **well** 熟 as well as ～と同様に be well -ed よく［十分に］～された 名井戸 oil well 油井
- **well-known** 形有名な
- **well-planned** 形計画性の高い
- **what if** もし～だったらどうなるだろうか
- **wheel** 名輪 Ferris wheel 大観覧車
- **whenever** 接～するたびに
- **whether** 接～であろうとなかろうと

- **whole** 形 全体の, すべての, 丸~ 名《the ~》全体, 全部 on the whole 全体的に見て
- **whom** 代 ①誰を[に] ②《関係代名詞》~するの人
- **whopping** 形 途方もない
- **widely** 副 広範囲にわたって
- **Wikileaks** 名 ウィキリークス《内部告発の機密情報を公開するウェブサイト》
- **wildlife** 名 野生生物
- **William H. Gates Senior** ウィリアム・H・ゲイツ・シニア《人名》
- **Willie Nelson** ウィリー・ネルソン《人名》
- **win** 動 勝つ
- **Windows** 名 ウィンドウズ《マイクロソフトのOSシリーズ、及びサービスブランド》
- **Windows Vista** ウィンドウズ・ヴィスタ《マイクロソフトのOS》
- **winning** 名《-s》賞金
- **within** 前 ~以内で, ~を越えないで
- **word** 熟 in other words すなわち, 言い換えれば
- **Word** 名 ワード《マイクロソフトのワープロソフト》
- **WordPerfect Corporation** ワードパーフェクト・コーポレーション《社名》
- **word-processing** 名 ワープロ, (パソコンでの)文書作成
- **work** 熟 at work 働いて, 仕事中で take time off work 仕事を休む work on ①~で機能する ②~に取り組む
- **worker** 名 労働者
- **world** 熟 in the world 世界で world of ~の世界
- **World Economic Forum** 世界経済協議会
- **World Health Organization** 世界保健機関《国連の専門機関》
- **World Wide Web** ワールド・ワイド・ウェブ, インターネット
- **worldwide** 形 世界規模の
- **worry** 熟 worry about ~のことを心配する be worried about (~のことで)心配している, ~が気かかる
- **worse** 形 より劣った get worse 悪化する
- **worst** 形《the ~》最も悪い, いちばんひどい
- **worth** 形 (~の)価値がある 名 価値
- **worthless** 形 価値のない
- **worthy** 形 価値のある
- **wrong with**《be -》~に欠陥がある

X

- **Xanadu** 名 ザナドゥ《映画『市民ケーン』(1941)に登場する、新聞王ケーンの未完の大豪邸》
- **Xanadu 2.0** ザナドゥ2.0《ビル・ゲイツ私邸の愛称》
- **Xbox** 名 エックスボックス《マイクロソフトの家庭用ゲーム機》
- **Xerox** 名 ゼロックス《社名》
- **Xerox Star** ゼロックス・スター《ゼロックスの業務用PC》

Y

- **Yale** 名 エール大学
- **year** 熟 for ~ years ~年間, ~年にわたって
- **yell** 動 わめく
- **yes-man** 名 追従者, イエスマン
- **yet** 熟 not yet まだ~してない
- **YouTube** 名 ユーチューブ《動画共有ポータルサイト》

Z

- **Zune** 图 ズーン《マイクロソフトが開発し、販売したポータブルメディアプレイヤー》

English Conversational Ability Test
国際英語会話能力検定

● E-CATとは…
英語が話せるようになるためのテストです。インターネットベースで、30分であなたの発話力をチェックします。

www.ecatexam.com

● iTEP®とは…
世界各国の企業、政府機関、アメリカの大学300校以上が、英語能力判定テストとして採用。オンラインによる90分のテストで文法、リーディング、リスニング、ライティング、スピーキングの5技能をスコア化。iTEP®は、留学、就職、海外赴任などに必要な、世界に通用する英語力を総合的に評価する画期的なテストです。

www.itepexamjapan.com

ラダーシリーズ
The Bill Gates Story ビル・ゲイツ・ストーリー

2017年12月7日　第1刷発行
2023年 7 月6日　第4刷発行

著　者　トム・クリスティアン

発行者　浦　晋亮

発行所　IBCパブリッシング株式会社
　　　　〒162-0804　東京都新宿区中里町29番3号
　　　　菱秀神楽坂ビル
　　　　Tel. 03-3513-4511　Fax. 03-3513-4512
　　　　www.ibcpub.co.jp

© IBC Publishing, Inc. 2017

印刷　中央精版印刷株式会社
装丁　伊藤 理恵
組版データ　Sabon Roman + Univers Bold

落丁本・乱丁本は、小社宛にお送りください。送料小社負担にてお取り替えいたします。本書の無断複写（コピー）は著作権法上での例外を除き禁じられています。

Printed in Japan
ISBN978-4-7946-0517-7